1–4 Petit doilies made with basics of crochet stitches (chain st, single crochet and double crochet). When you become good at the work, make pochettes for your friends.
Designed by Michiko Inoue.
Instructions on pages 4 to 7.

1-4 Refreshing square mesh

Shown on page 2 and 3.

You'll need: DMC art 980 COTON LUSTRE C.B. 1. 10g saffron pink (8717). 2.3. 20g each of cream (8764) and pale green (8736). Satin 16.5 cm×28 cm. 4. A bit of pink (8739). Satin 10 cm×18 cm. Steel crochet hook D (2.0 mm).
Finished size: 1. 21 cm×17 cm. 2·3. 14.5 cm×14 cm. 4.8 cm×9 cm.

Instructions: Make a large pochette same as a petit doily. Work referring to chart. Fold the lace inside out and join with sc to complete large and small pochettes. Make an inner bag and join with lace. Pass braid through the 1st row of edging and pull. See page 32 to make an inner bag.

Making work No. 1.

(Refer to chart on page 6.)

● Hold hook and thread correctly.

Holding thread

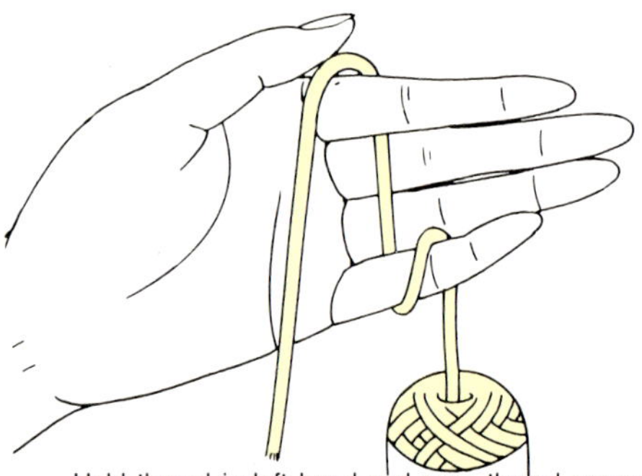

Hold thread in left hand and pass thread around the little finger, then take it under the ring and middle fingers, and then over the index finger to control taking thread from ball.

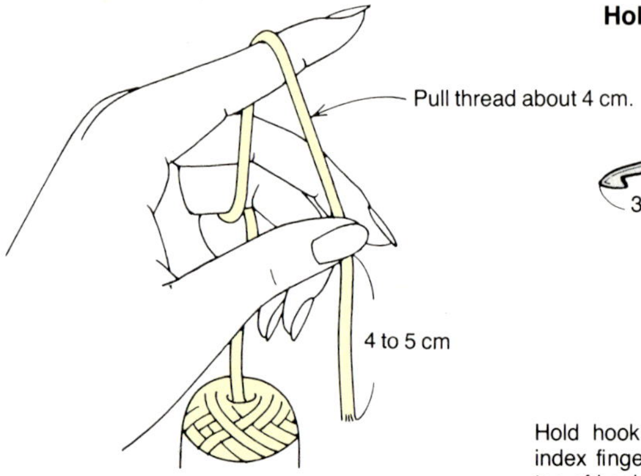

Raise index finger to be able to move according to gauge.

Holding hook

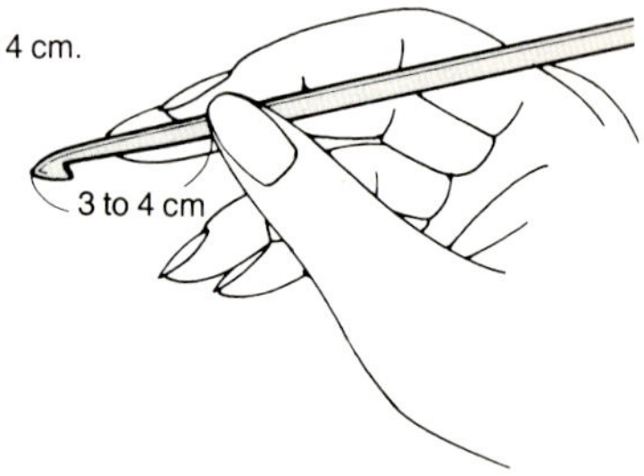

Hold hook on right hand. Place hook between index finger and thumb and put middle finger on top of hook sloping below. Put middle finger lightly to allow free movement because it holds the thread on the hook.

Chain stitch ○

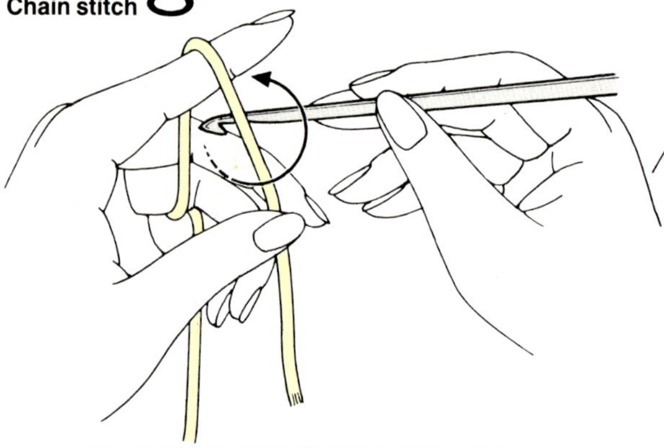

Place hook on the opposite side and turn (arrow).

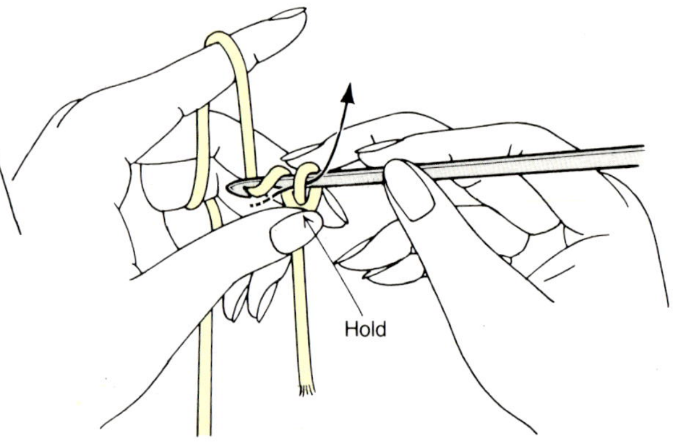

Catch thread with hook and draw up.

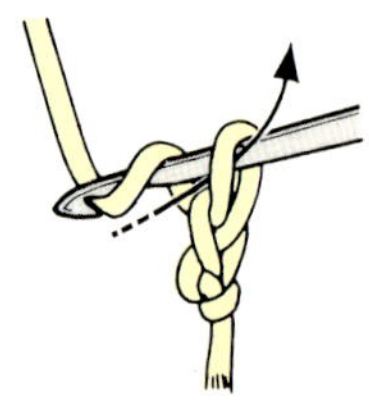

Work ch 52 drawing up sts in same manner.

● Work row 1.

Double crochet

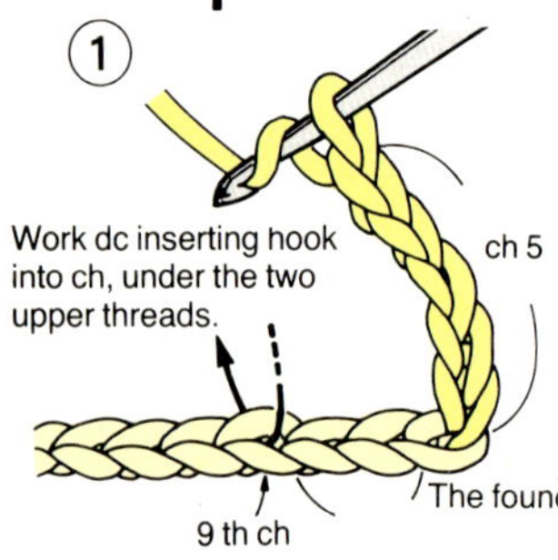

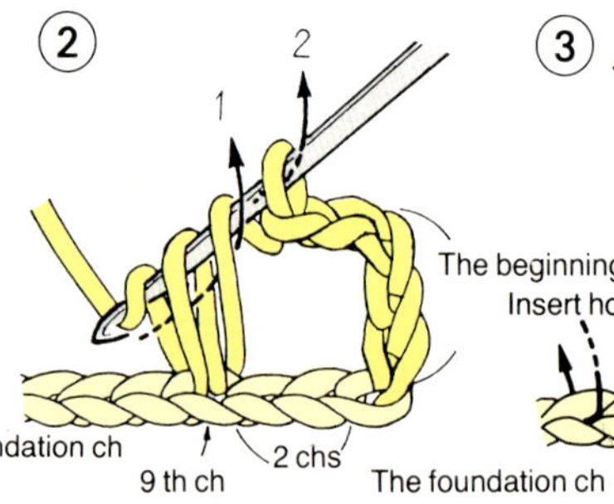

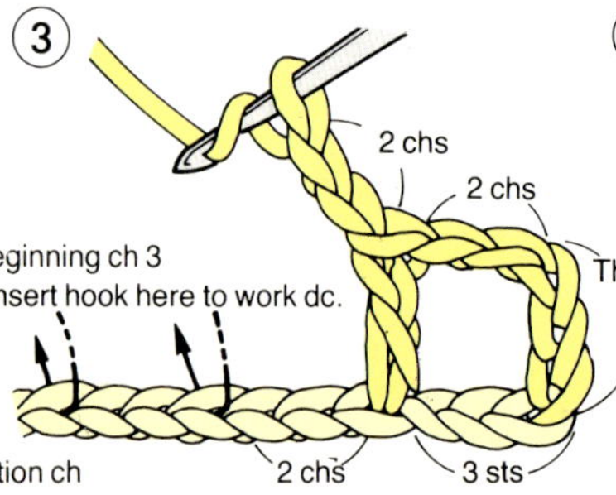

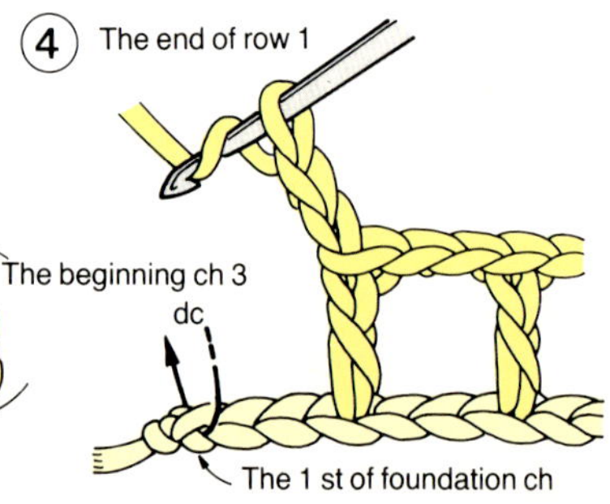

● **Work row 2.**

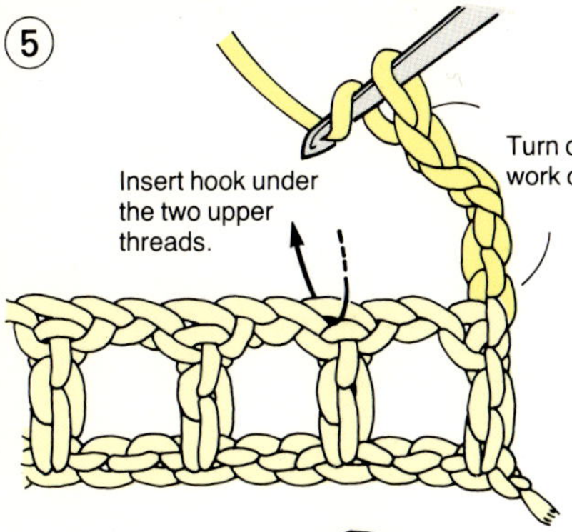

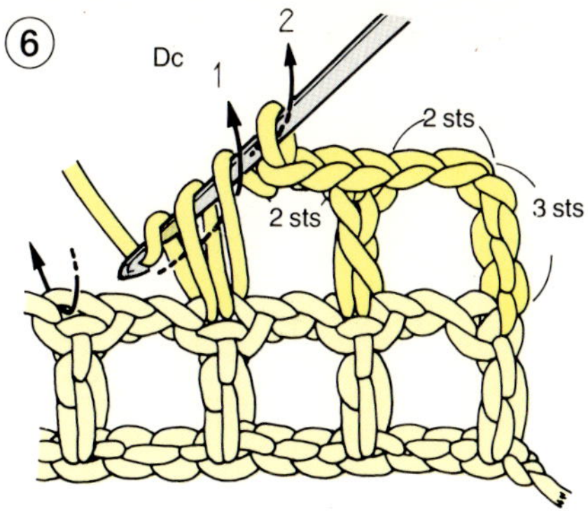

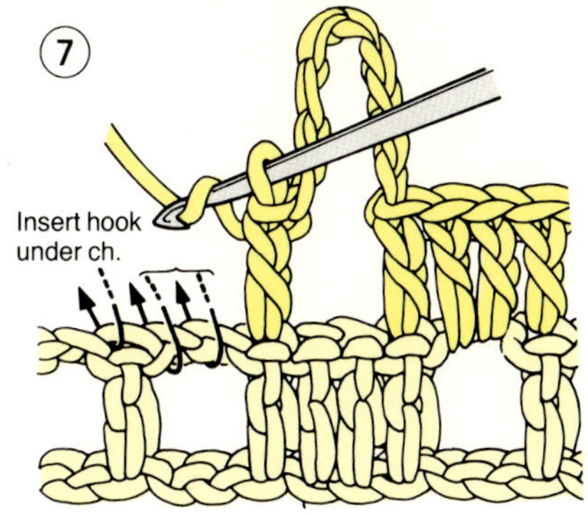

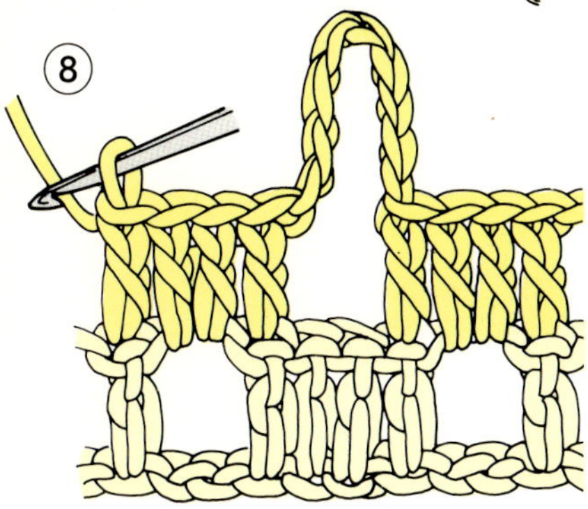

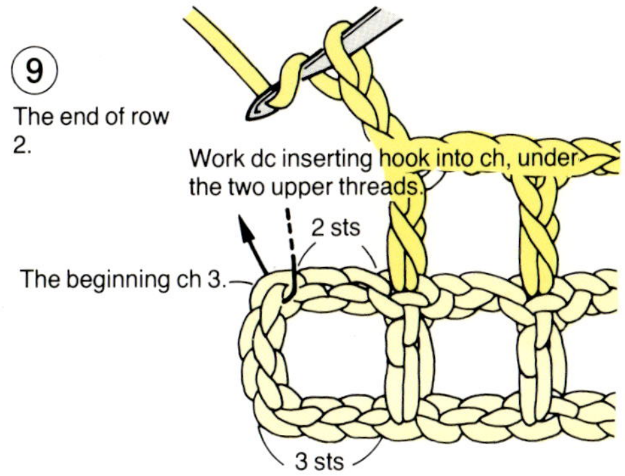

● **Work row 3.**

Single crochet +

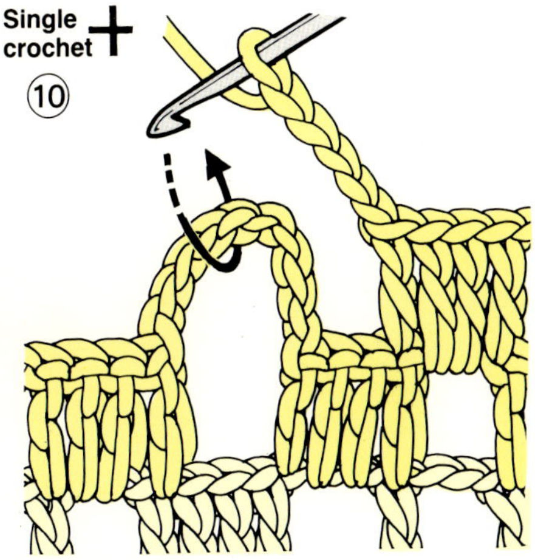

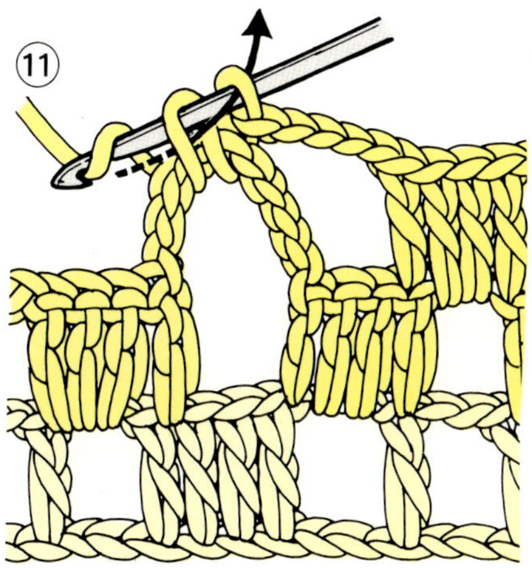

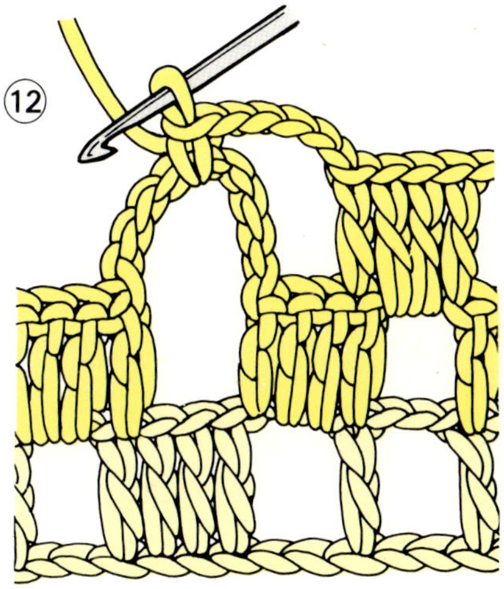

● **Work edging.**

On row 1, work the beginning ch 1 and sc inserting hook (arrows).

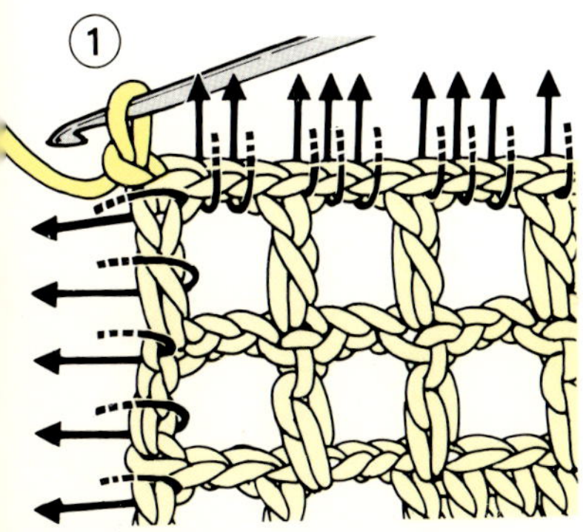

Slip stitch

Work sl st in the beginning st.

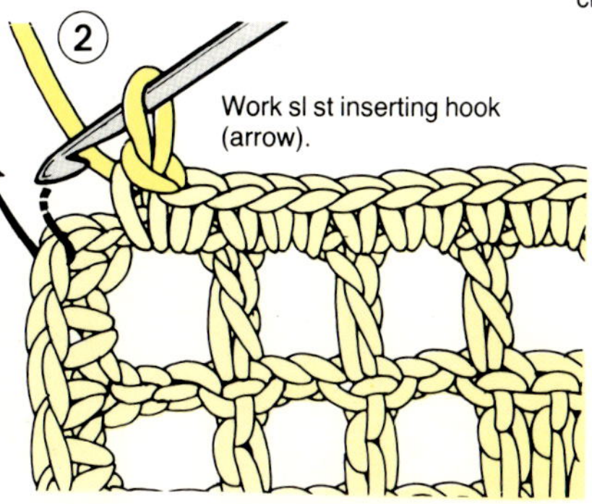

Sl st-picot with 3-ch

On row 2, insert hook into the third ch and draw up 2 loops at a time.

Work ch 3 and sc as shown in chart.

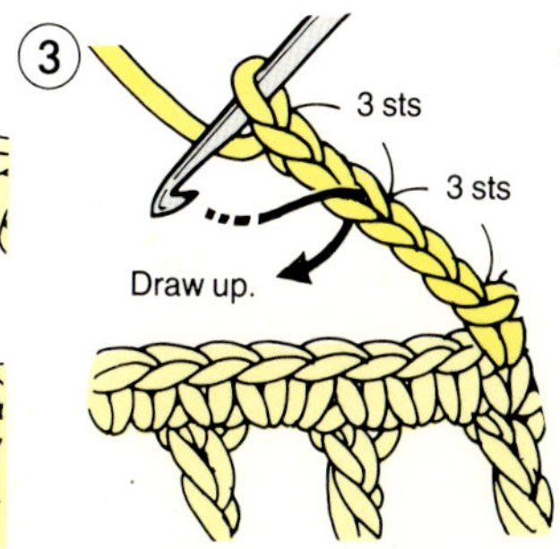

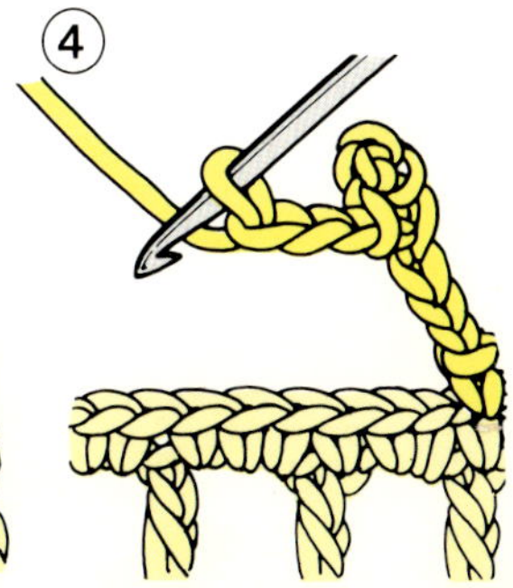

Chart of petit doily

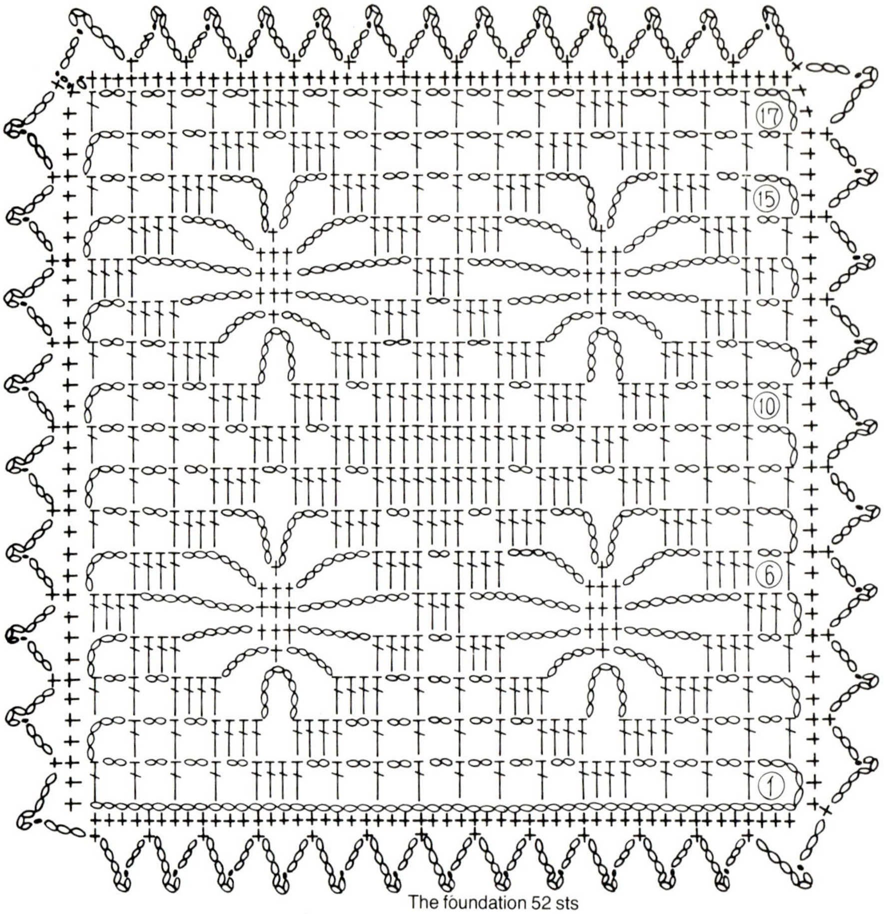

The foundation 52 sts

Making work Nos. 2 to 4.

● Join both sides.

(Joining with sc)

Fold at the bottom inside out and work sc inserting hook into both sides (arrows).

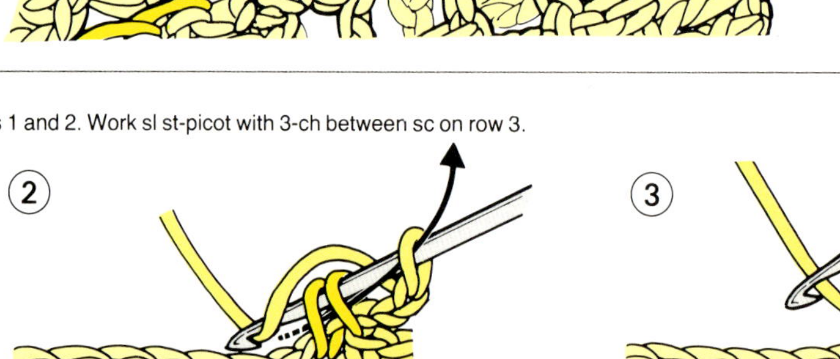

● Work edging.

After joining with sc, turn over and work square mesh on rows 1 and 2. Work sl st-picot with 3-ch between sc on row 3.

①

Insert hook under two upper threads.

②

③

● **Make braid.**

Braid in three strands.

Make braid as shown below and pass it through on a pochette.

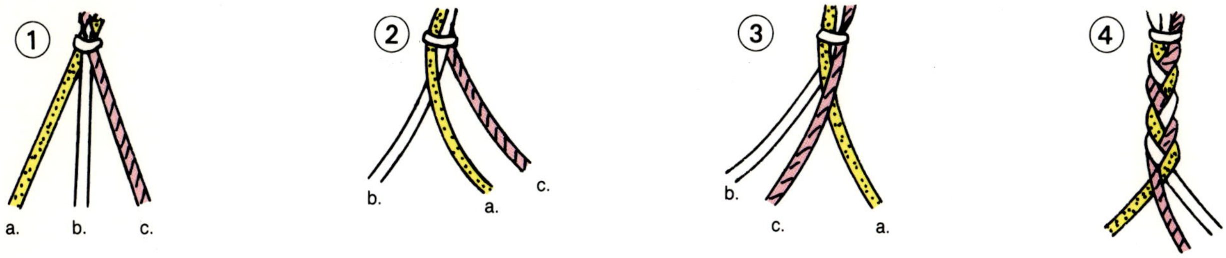

Chart of pochette (large) 2·3

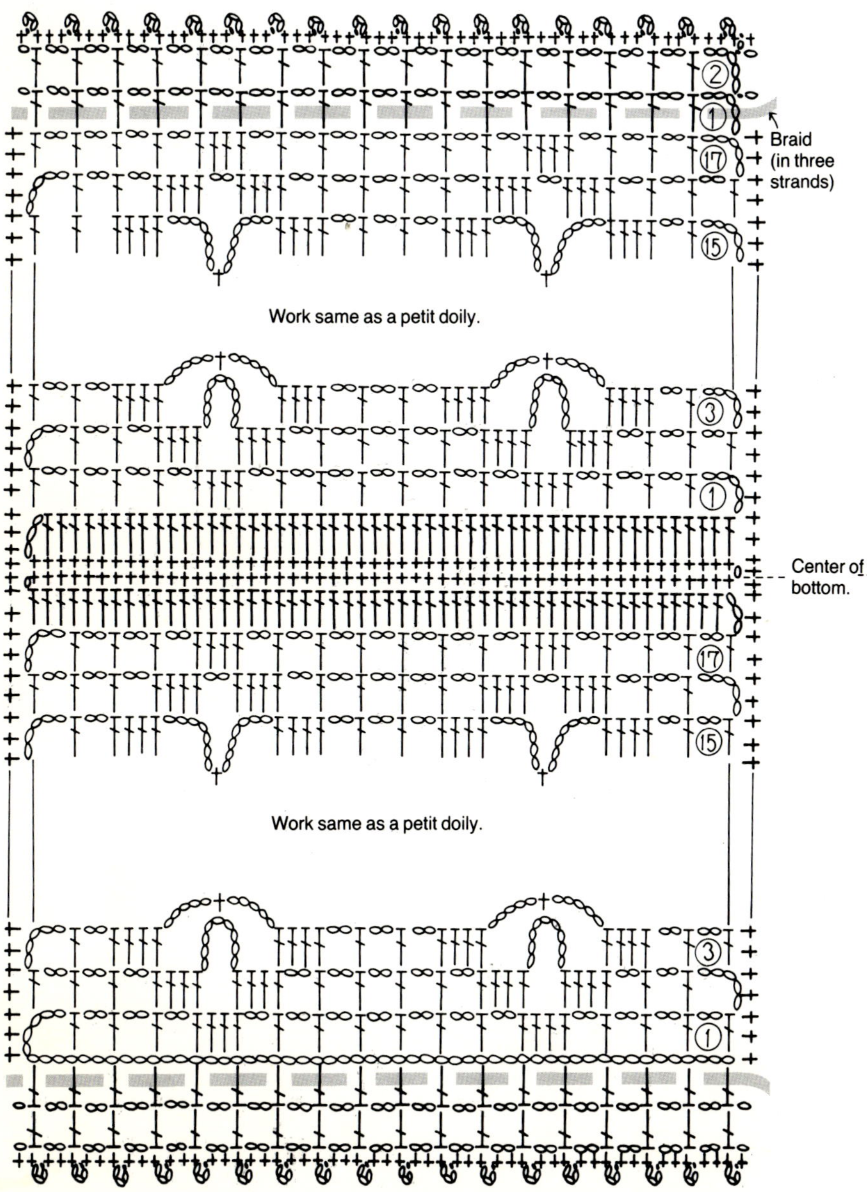

Chart of pochette (small) 4

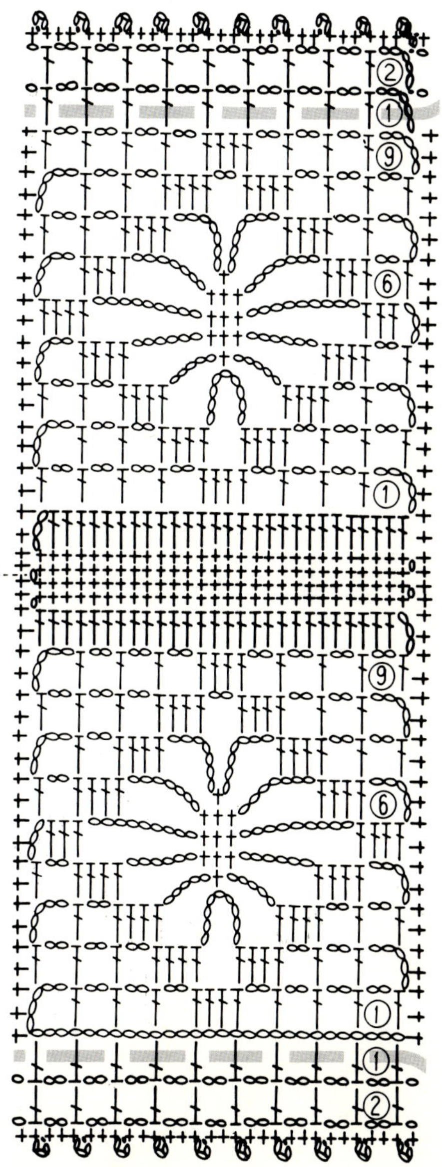

5–8 Purse with simple square mesh work

Shown on page 9.

You'll need: 5–7. DMC art 980 COTON LUSTRE C.B. 20g each of sky blue (8730), beige (8775), and yellow (8766). 8. Loose twisted crochet cotton (thick type) 50g yellow (8721). Sky blue, beige and reddish yellow satin 18 cm x 34 cm. 200 cm cord. Steel crochet hook D (2.0 mm) and E (2.5 mm).
Finished size: 5–7. 16 cm×19 cm. 8. 23 cm×25 cm.
Instructions: Work ch 41. Rows 1 and 2: Work around with sc. Rows 3 and 4: Work tr increasing sts at both sides. Rows 5–17: Ch 4 at the beginning and repeat "ch 2, 1 tr" around until row 17 in same manner. Row 18: Ch 1 and repeat around with "1 sc, ch 9". Make an inner bag as shown on page 32 and join with lace. Pass braid through on the 15th row. 8. Work ch 108 to form ring. Repeat "1 dc, ch 2" until row 19 in same manner. Row 20: Work same as row 18. Fasten off sts of the foundation ch.

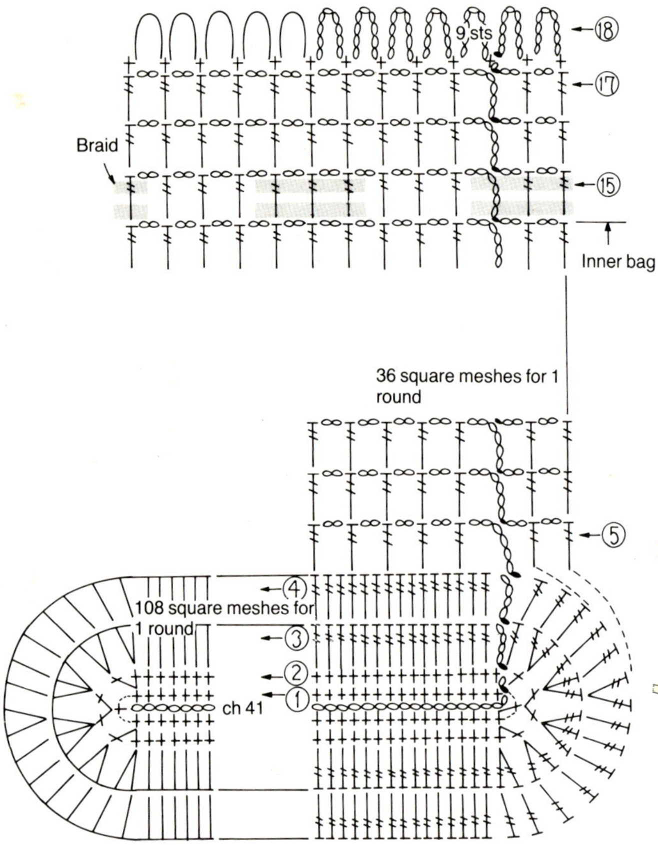

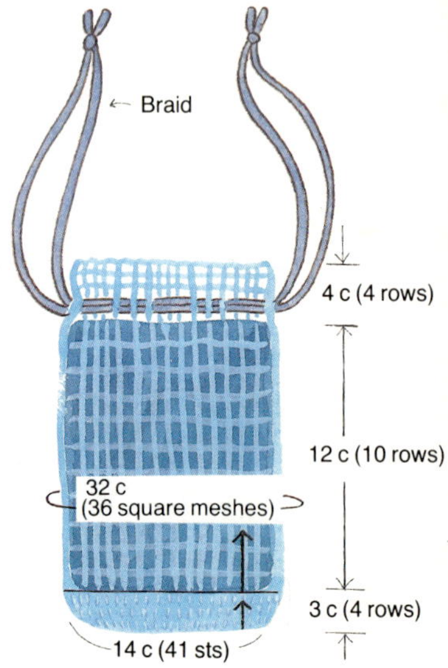

Fastening off sts

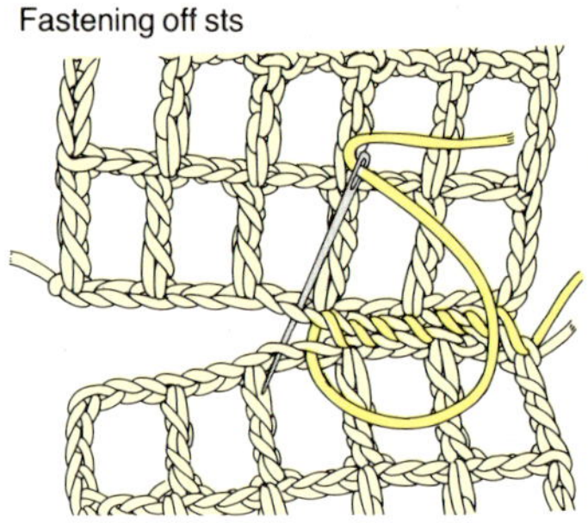

Treble crochet (tr) enlarged

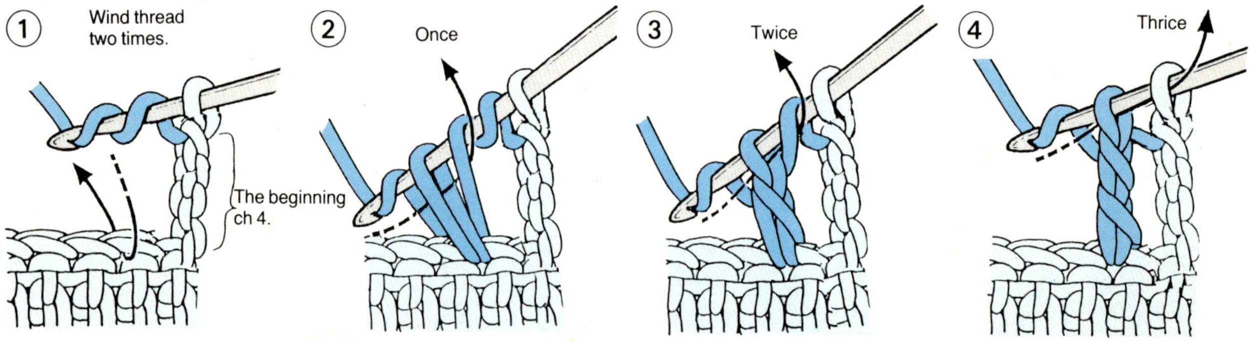

Basic

5–8 It is useful to have any number of purses with simple square mesh. You can make any size you like, changing threads or stitches slightly.
Designed by Hideko Nagashima.
Instructions on page 8.

Daisy

● I love a daisy.

9–15 Variations of accessories

Shown on page 11.

Chart of flower (large)

Chart of flower (small)

Note: In case of changing color of large and small flowers, work in same color on rows 1 and 2, and in another color on row 3.

Making flower (small)

①

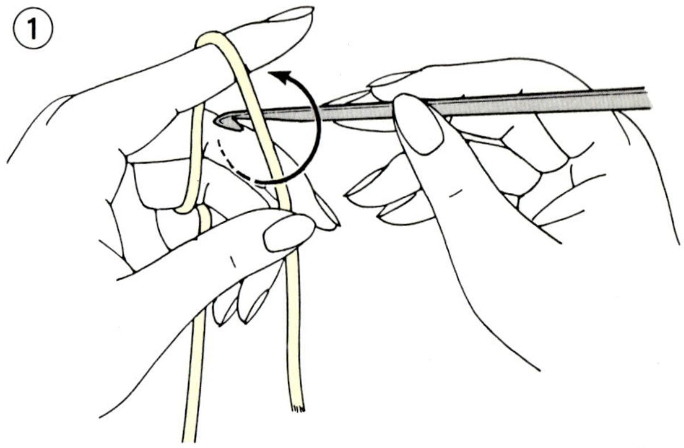

②

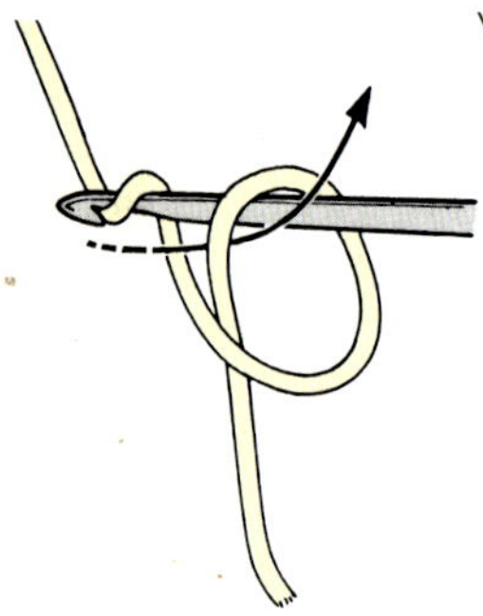

③

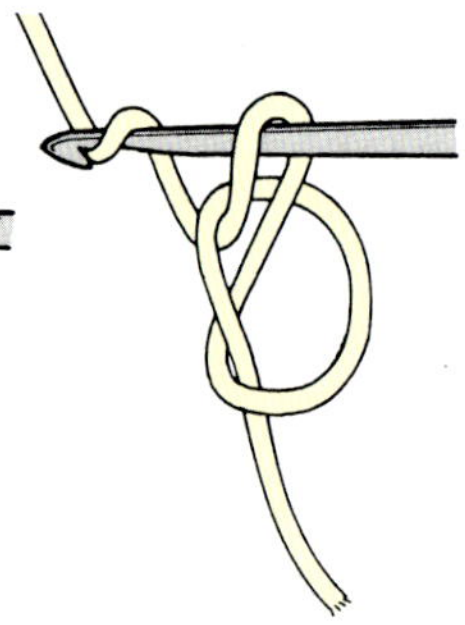

④ Row 1

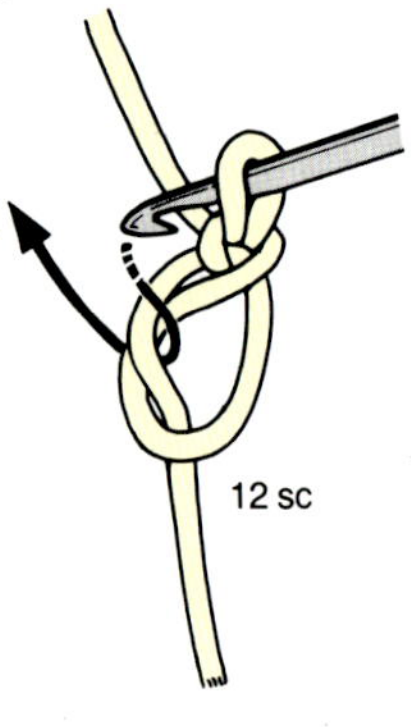

⑤

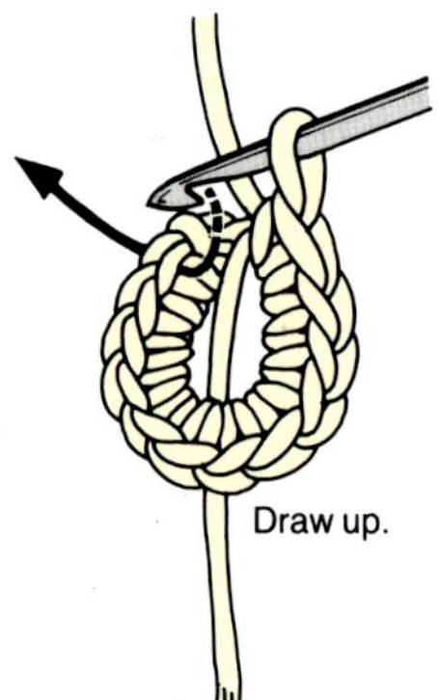

⑥ Row 2

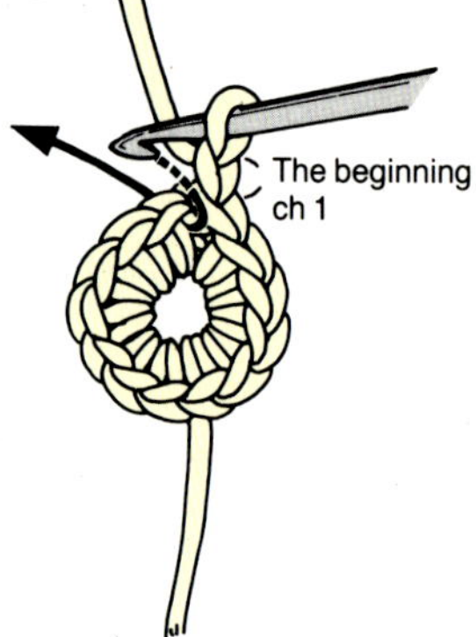

⑦

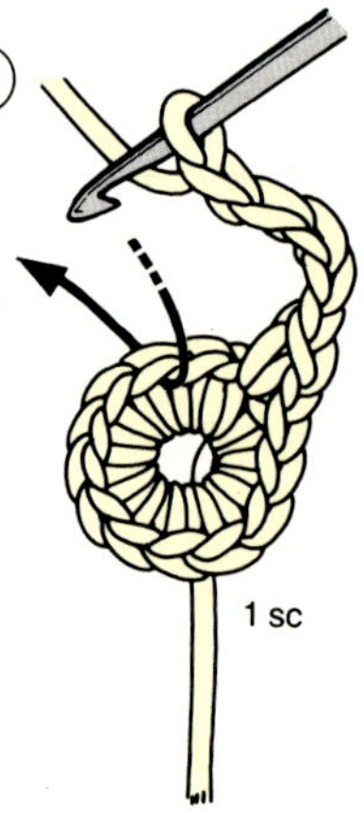

⑧

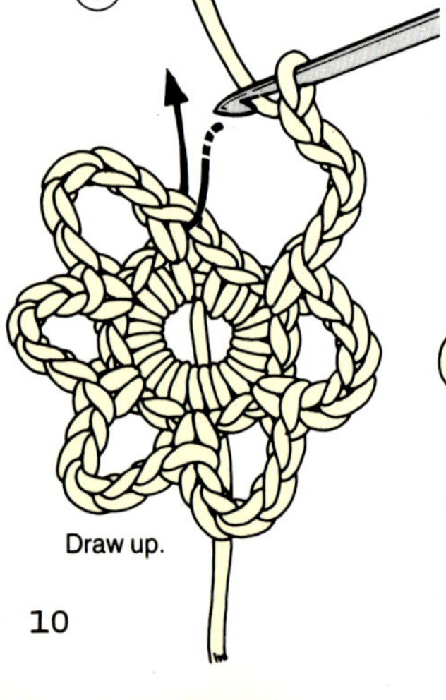

⑨ Row 3

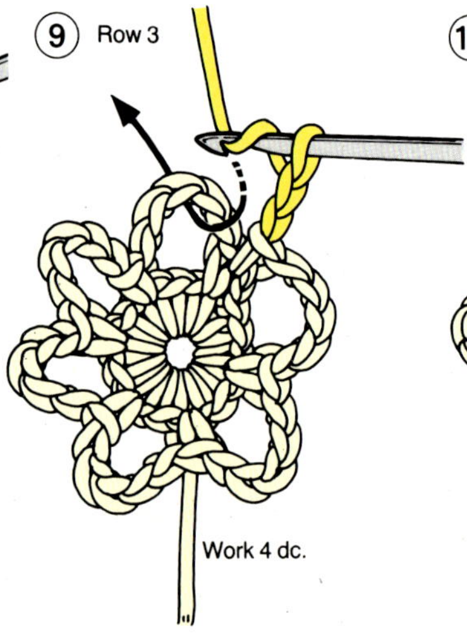

⑩

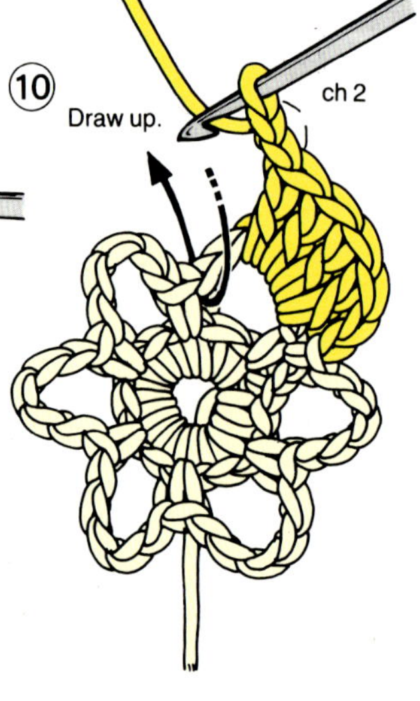

⑪

Daisy

9–15 Make many pretty flowers by changing colors or one on top of the other. It is cute to have a bouquet or a brooch with ribbon. Try to design your original.
Designed by Hitomi Tamura.
Instructions on page 10.

You'll need: Loose twisted crochet cotton (thick type) are used to make flowers, Nos. 9–18. As these flowers can be made with a bit of thread, use the balance from other works. Steel crochet hook F (3.0 mm).

Finished size: Flower motif (large) 4.5 cm in diameter. (small) 4 cm in diameter.

Instructions: Work in same manner to make any motif. Make large or small motifs as you prefer. To make a motif on top of the other, put the small one on the large one. If changing color, work in same color on rows 1 and 2, and in another color on row 3. Use beads and ribbon to complete acute one.

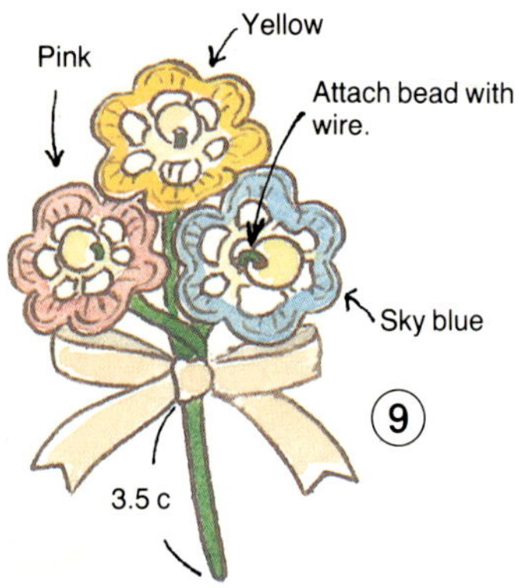

⑨

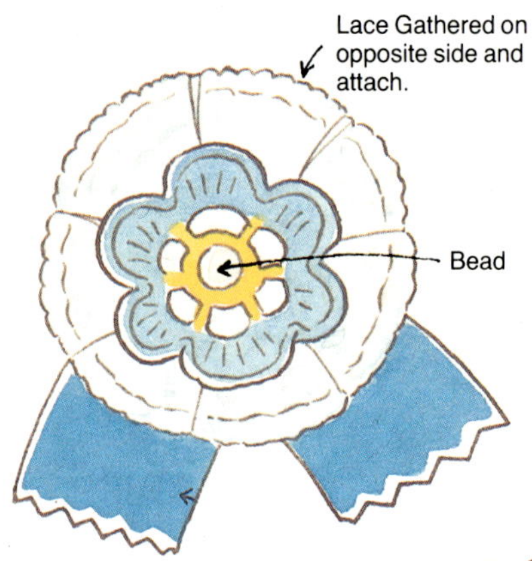

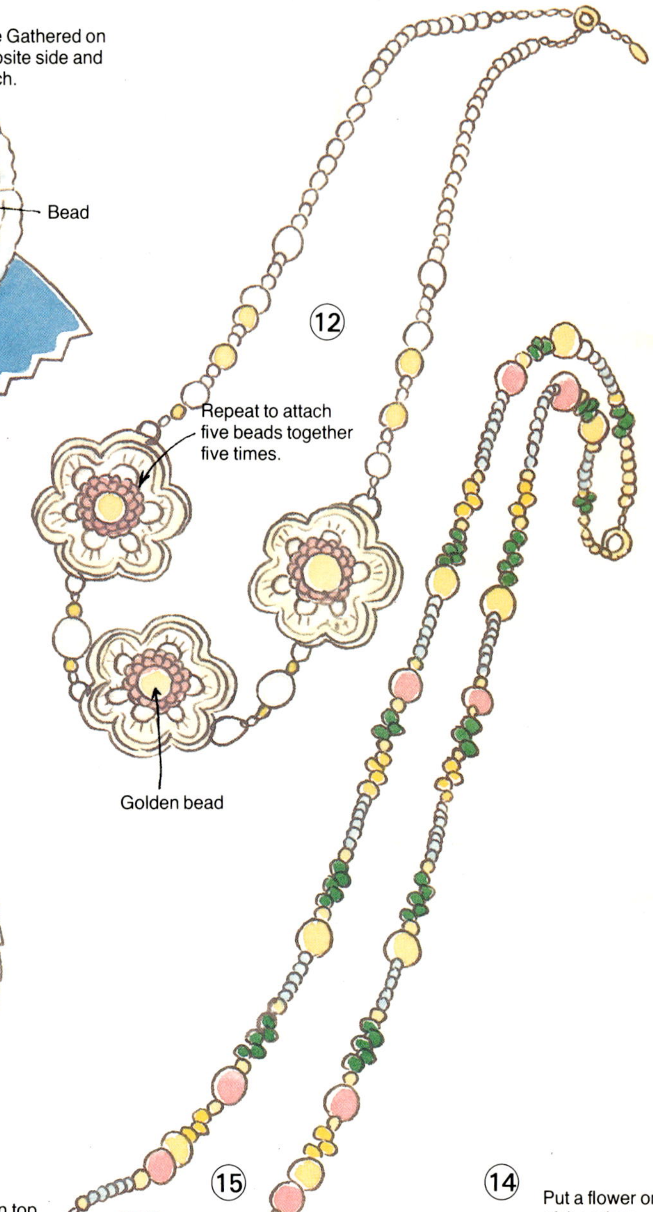

⑫ ⑮

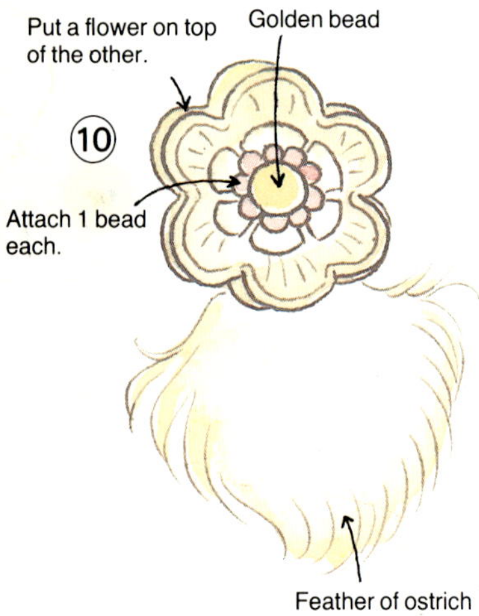

⑩

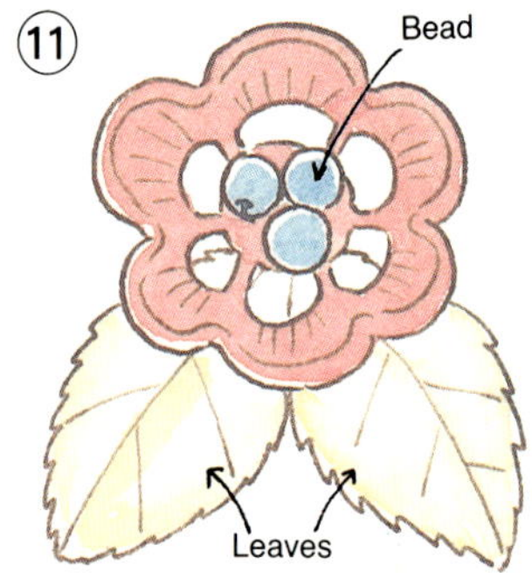

⑪

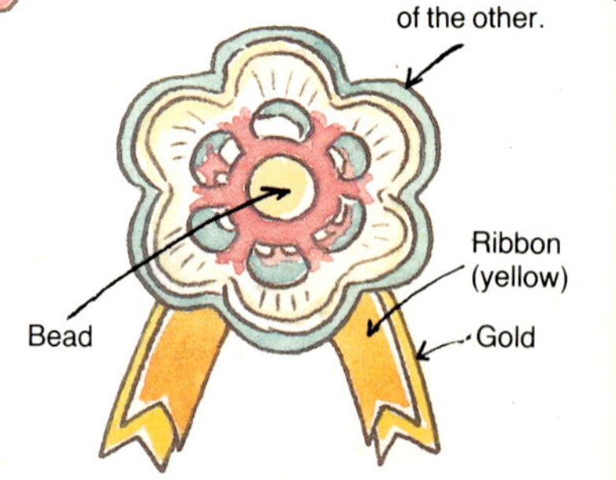

⑭

Daisy

16–18 Simple frame becomes lovely with flowers. It is also nice to put flowers on a cardigan or socks. Enjoy making up with a lot of flowers.
Designed by Hitomi Tamura.
Instructions on page 12.

19 Petit doily of daisy

Shown on page 15.

You'll need: DMC art 980 COTON LUSTRE C.B. 10g pink (8739). Steel crochet hook D (2.0 mm).
Finished size: 17 cm in diameter.
Instructions: Motif Work ch 6 to form ring. Row 1: Ch 1 at the beginning and work 12 sc. Row 2: Ch 1 and repeat "1 sc, ch 5". Row 3: Repeat around with "ch 2, 2 dc, ch 1, 2 dc, ch 2, 1 sl st". Join other motifs with sl st at 2 points on row 3 except the first motif. Centerpiece Work in same manner on rows 1 and 2. Row 3: Ch 1 and repeat around with "1 sc, ch 3, 1 sl st, ch 3" joining with six motifs. Edging Row 1: Ch 1 and repeat "1 sc, ch 6, 1 sc, ch 6, 1 tr". Rows 2–5: Work net st increasing the number of ch.

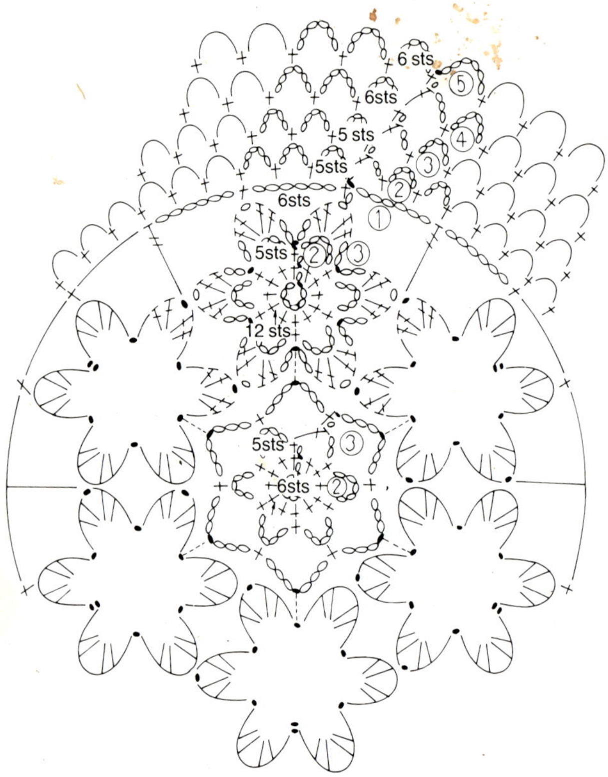

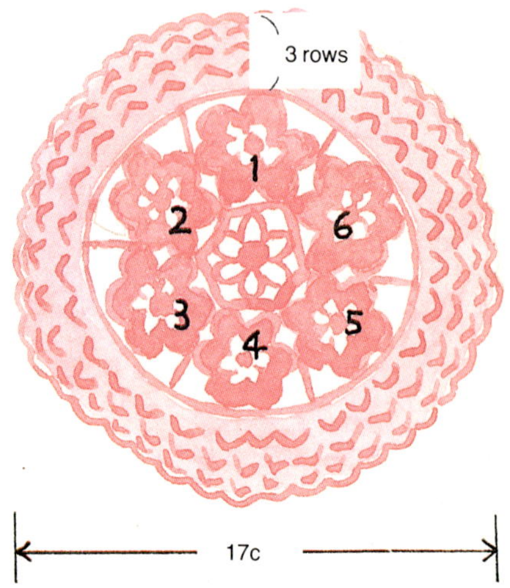

Joining motifs

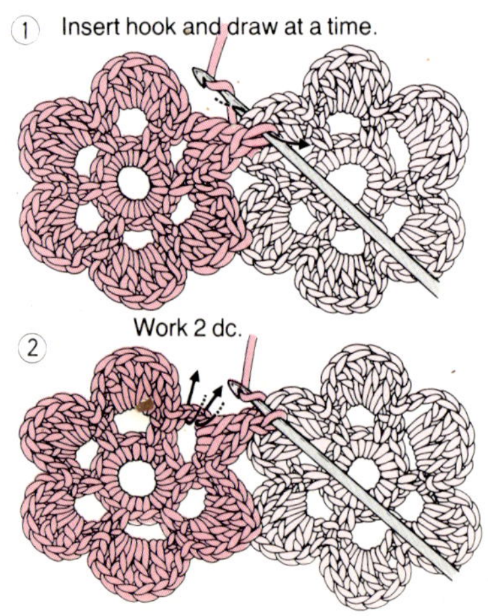

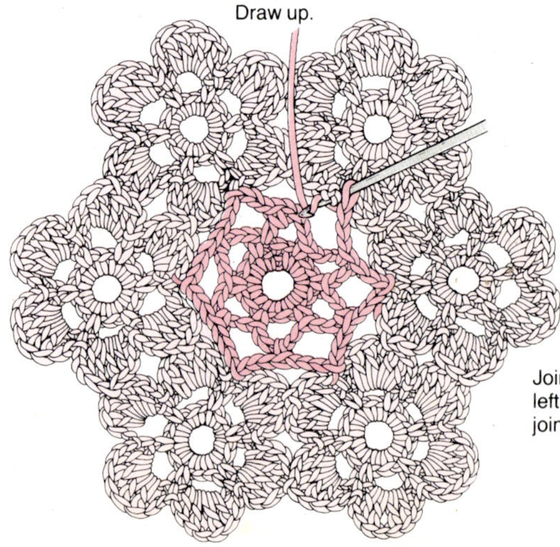

Join 6 motifs as shown in left and work centerpiece joining with outer motifs.

19

Daisy

19 Make a doily joining six flower motifs. The work becomes elegant with net st of edging. Designed by Sumiko Nomura. Instructions on page 14.

Collar & Tie

Fashionable crochet lace

20–23 Collar and tie

Shown on page 17.

You'll need: DMC art 980 COTON LUSTRE C.B. 20. 20g white. Ribbon 0.6 cm wide. Beads 0.3 cm in diameter. 21. 20g white. Ribbon 0.6 cm wide, 76 cm. 22. A bit of white. 108 white and 15 golden beads. Lace 4 cm in wide, 9 cm. 23. A bit of pink (8739) and white. 12 small blue and 8 pink beads. Steel crochet hook D (2.0 mm).

Finished size: 20. 21. 40 cm in inside and 70 cm in outside diameter of collar. 7 cm wide. 22. 23. 7 cm×4 cm.

Instructions: Thread all beads in advance and work with each bead as shown in chart.

20

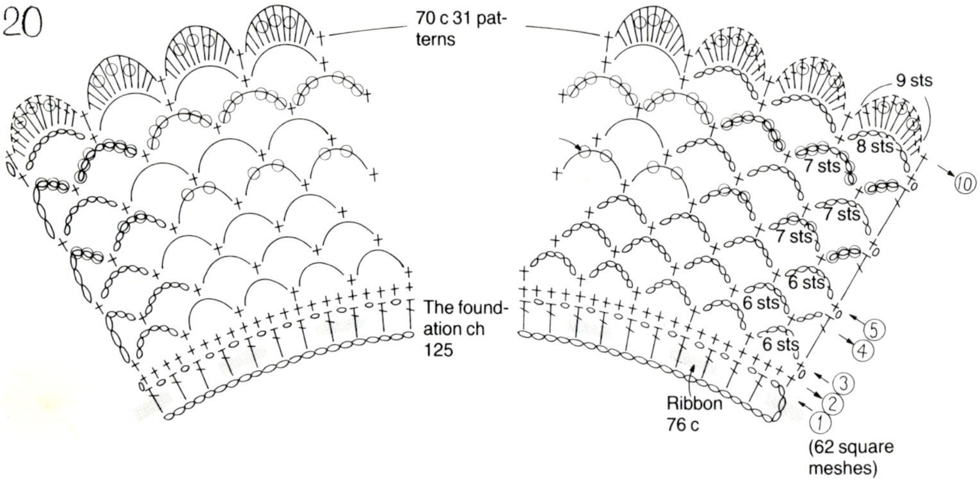

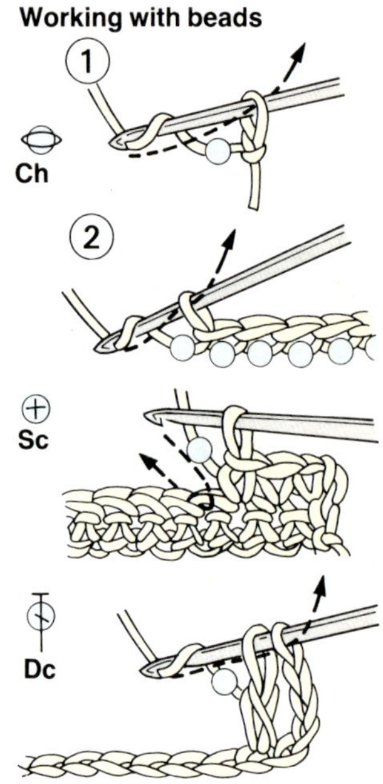

21

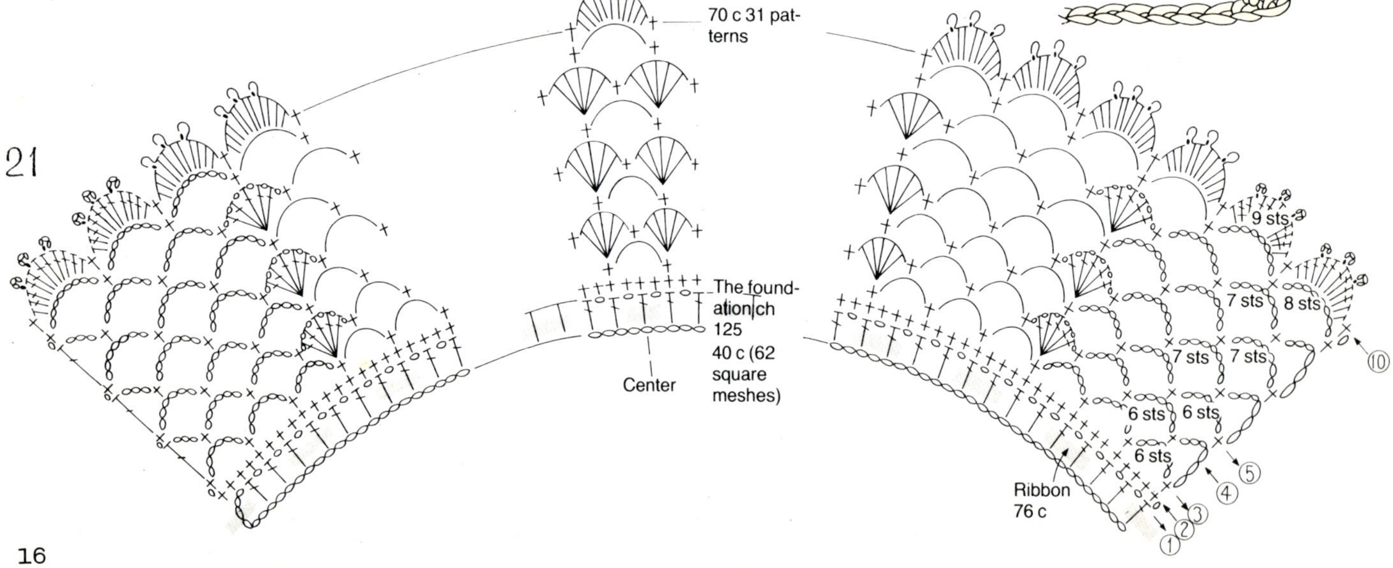

Collar & Tie

20, 21 Simple net st with beads or shell st. Collar of gentle lace will match well a romantic girl.
22, 23 Easy-to-make, straight shape ties become fashionable with beads or lace. These are nice to wear with your blouses.
Designed by Hitomi Tamura.
Instructions on page 16 and 50.

Doily. Doilies varied in size

24·25 Delightful color doilies

Shown on page 19.

You'll need: DMC art 980 COTON LUSTRE C.B. 30g white. 10g purple, yellow, green blue and pink gradation. Steel crochet hook No. 4 (1.75 mm).

Finished size: 24. 34 cm in diameter. 25. 17 cm in diameter.

Instructions: 24. Work the beginning ch 3 and 22 dc in a loop. Row 2: Ch 3 and repeat "ch 1, 1 dc" then ch 1, sl st at the end. Row 3: Ch 3, 1 dc and repeat around with "ch 1, 2 dc". Row 4: Ch 2, 1 dc and repeat "ch 4, 2-dc cluster". Rows 5 and 6: Work net st increasing the number of ch. Rows 7–17: Work net st and patterns referring to chart. Use gradation color thread on row 7 and 13. 25. Work in same manner as No. 24 from rows 1 to 7 and then work one more row as shown below to complete.

24

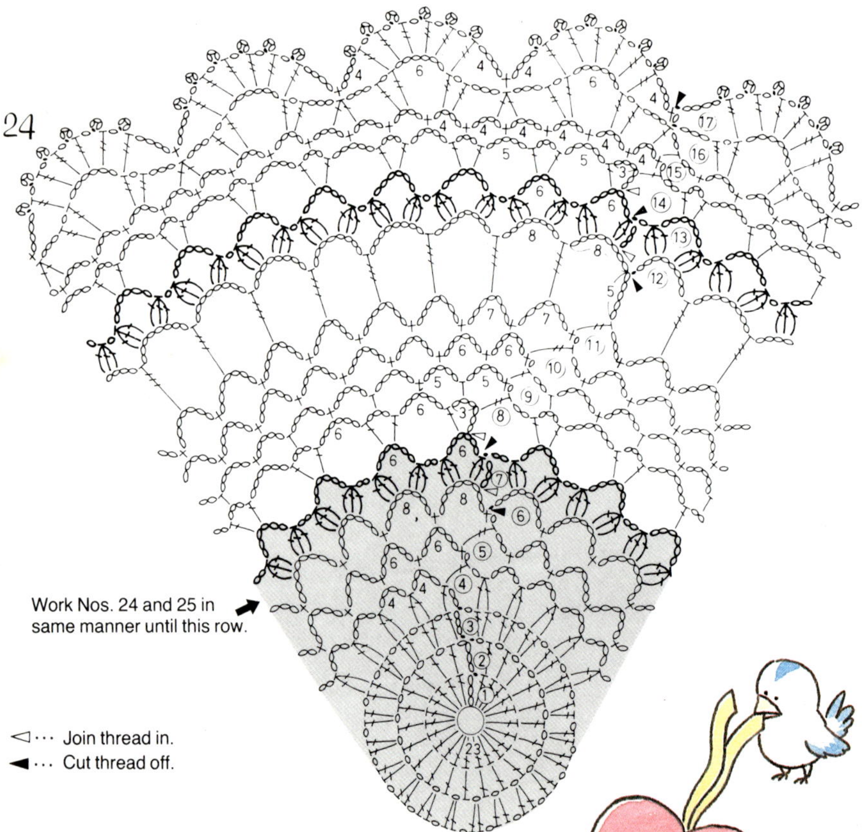

Work small one at first.

25

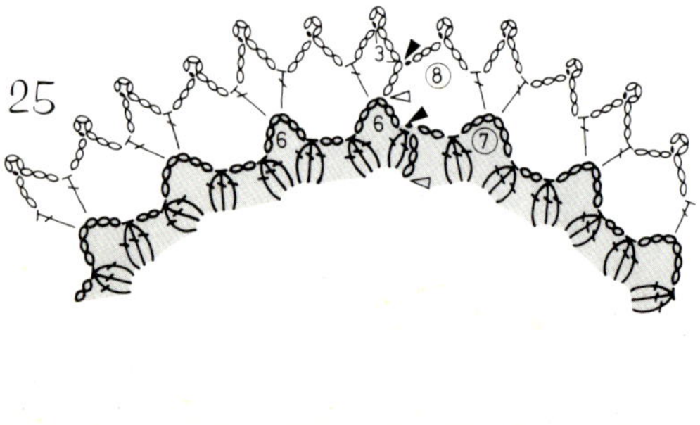

25

24

Doily

24, 25 After finishing a small doily, try to make a large one. Your work will be easier as it will be the same for the center. Designed by Kyoko Kawashima.

Instructions on page 18.

26·27 Sweet doilies

Shown on page 21.

You'll need: DMC art 980 COTON LUSTRE C.B. 15g white. 16g pink gradation. Steel crochet hook No. 4 (1.75 mm)

Finished size: 26. 29 cm in diameter. 27. 16 cm in diameter.

Instructions: 26. Row 1: Work the beginning ch 3 and 23 dc in a loop, then sl st to form ring. Rows 2–5: Work square meshes increasing the number of ch between dc. Row 6: Ch 1 and repeat around with "1 sc, sl st picot with 3 ch, 1 sc, ch 4". Rows 7-11: Work around with square meshes checking the number of ch sts. Row 12: Work same as row 6. Rows 13 and 14: Work around with dtr checking the number of ch sts. Rows 15–17: Work patterns referring to chart. Use gradation color on rows 6, 12, 15, 16 and 17. 27. Work in same manner from rows 1 to 5 and work 4 rows more.

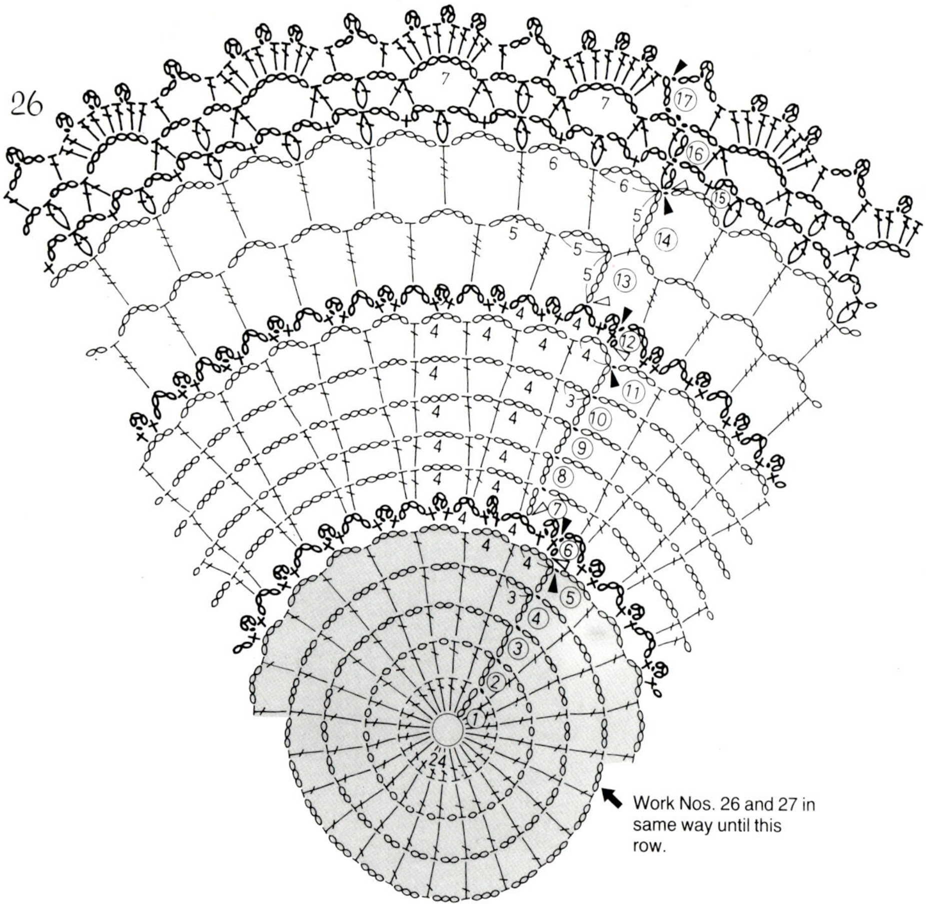

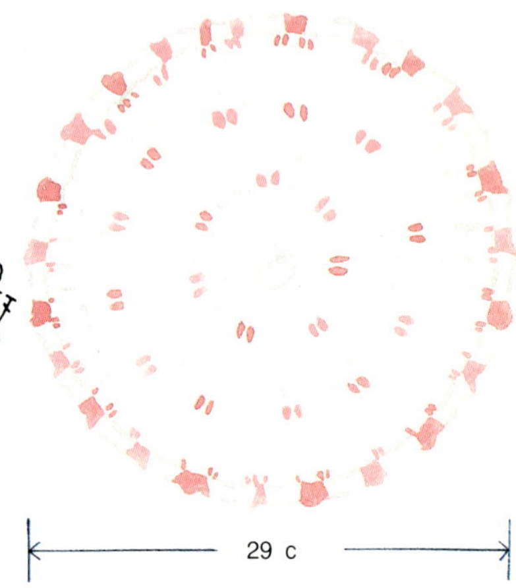

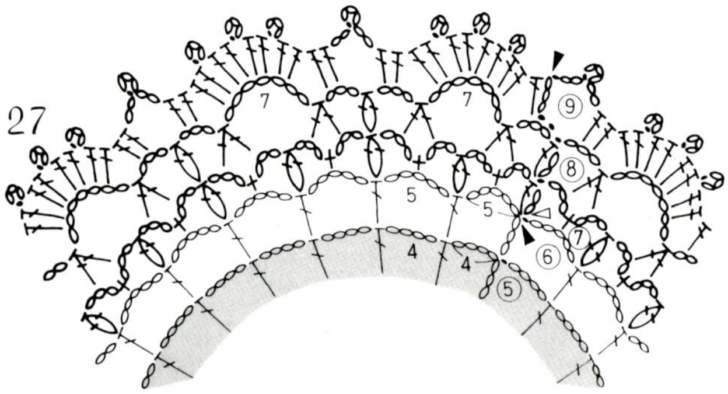

◁ ··· Join thread in.

◀ ··· Cut thread off.

Doily

26, 27 Sweet doilies can be imagined to give off a whiff of flowers and tenderness. Place on a dressing table or a side table.
Designed by Kyoko Kawashima.
Instructions on page 20.

Edging. Fancy edging variations

28–33 Edging for handkerchieves

Shown on page 23.

You'll need: 10g each of yellow (8721), pink (8739), red (8770), purple (8711), blue (8773) and green (8736). Handkerchief 33 cm×33 cm. Steel crochet hook D (2.0 mm).

Finished size: 28-33. 36 cm×36 cm.

Instructions: First put marks every 1 cm, 0.5 cm inside from the edge, on Nos. 28, 31, 32 and 33. Put marks every 0.7 cm in same way for Nos. 29 and 30. And then work sc.

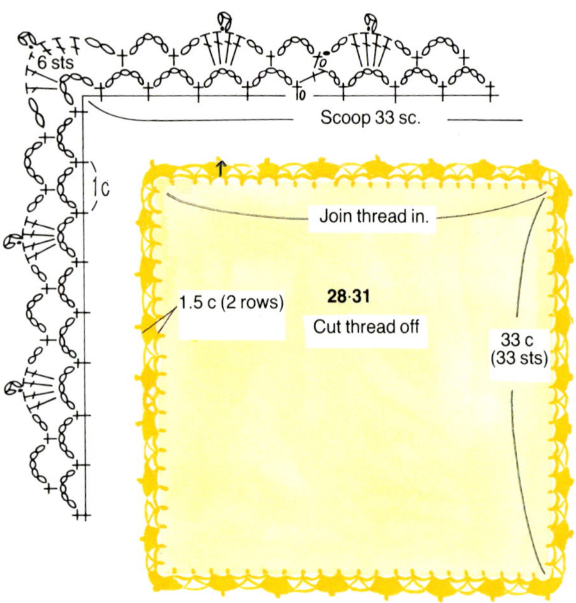

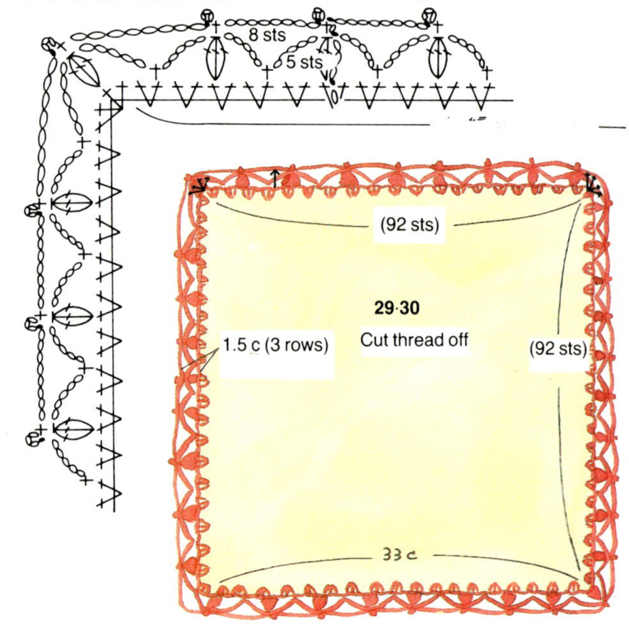

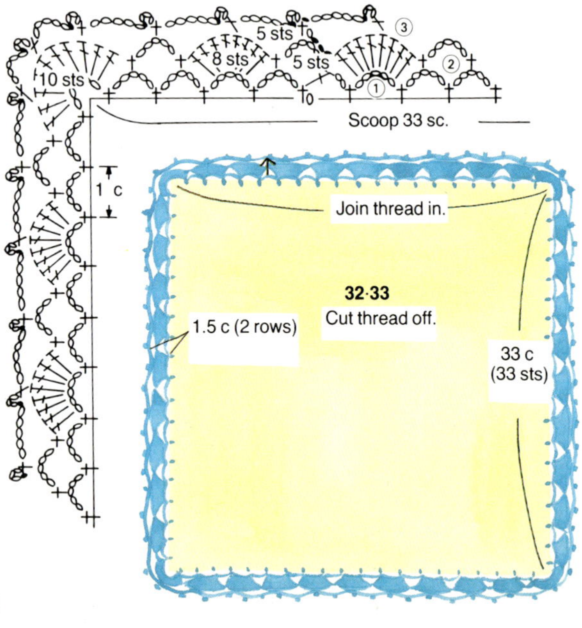

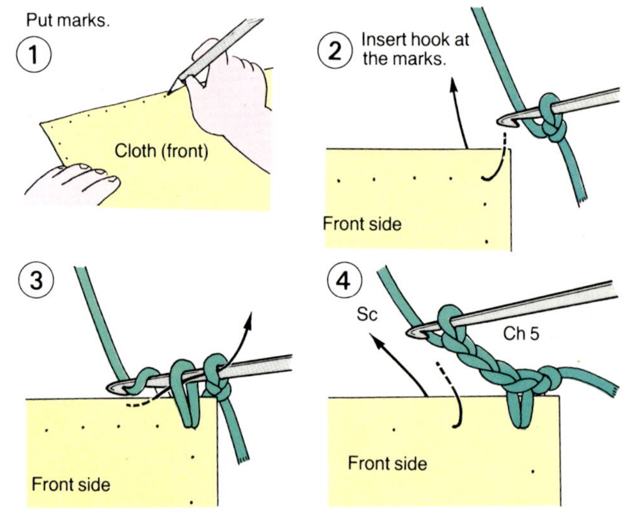

Edging

28–33 Colorful edging makes white handkerchieves gorgeous. Gentle crochet lace shows your personality.
Designed by Kimiko Ozawa.
Instructions on page 22.

34–36 Attractive handy baskets and pincushion

Shown on page 26.

You'll need: Large basket DMC art 980 COTON LUSTRE C.B. 20g dark pink (8771) and a bit of golden thread. Cotton print 32 cm x 28 cm. Quilted cloth 17 cm×23 cm. Ribbon 0.7 cm wide, 30 cm. Rattan basket 15 cm×21 cm and 8 cm deep. Small basket: DMC art 980 COTON LUSTRE C.B. a bit of dark pink (8771). Cotton print 22 cm×23 cm. 2 each of flower-shaped spangles and beads. Rattan basket 7.5 cm in diameter and 3.5 cm deep. Small basket for pincushion DMC art 980 COTON LUSTRE C.B. a bit of dark pink (8771) and white. Cotton print 17 cm×17 cm. Rattan basket 7.5 cm in diameter and 3.5 cm deep. Steel crochet hook D (1.50 mm).

Finished size: See the illustration.

Instructions: Work braid according to the sizes. Make each basket referring to illustration.

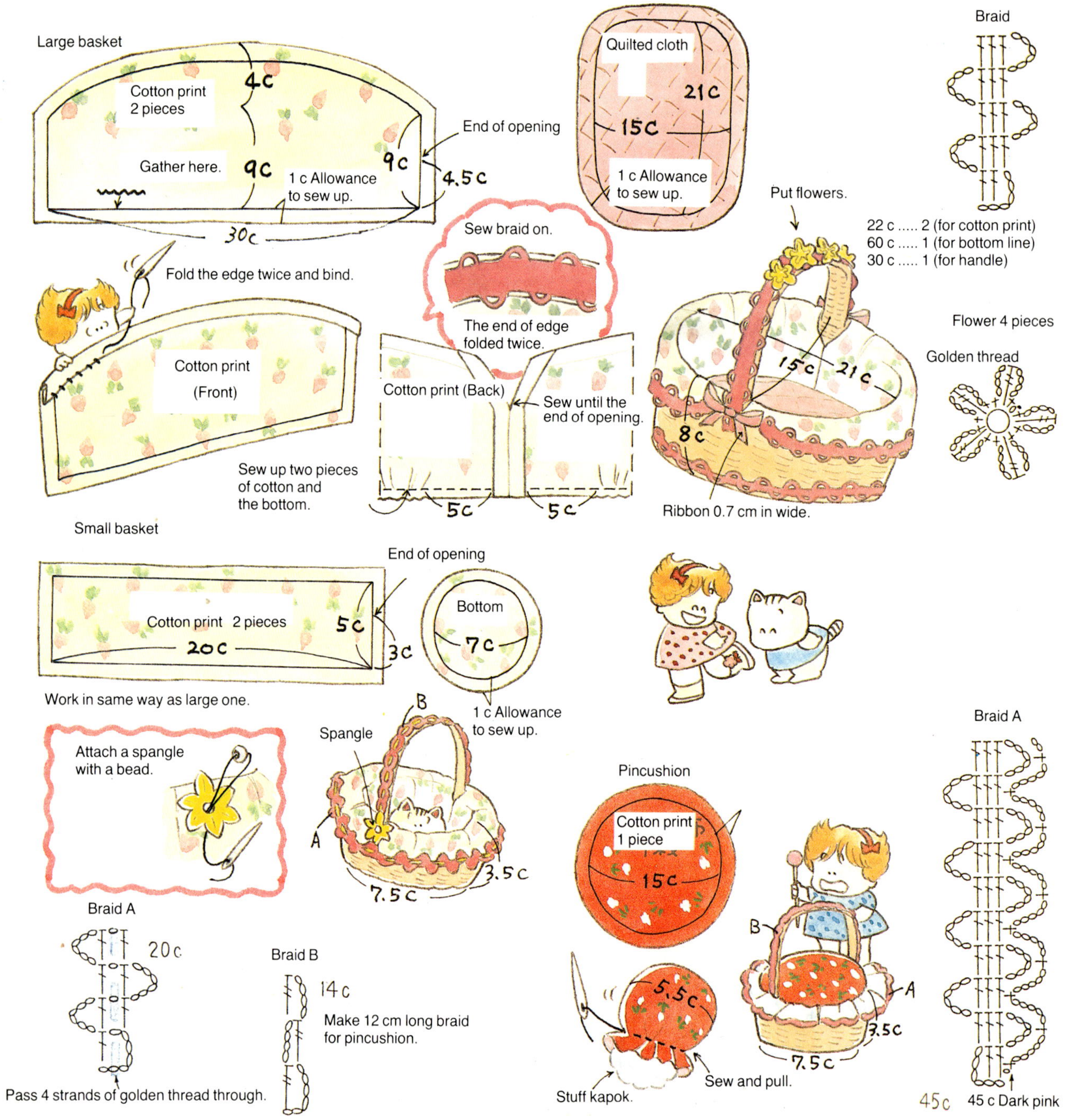

37–39 Dreamy petit cushions

Shown on page 27.

You'll need: 37. DMC art 980 COTON LUSTRE C.B. 10g white. a bit of blue (8773) and green (8736). Ribbon 2.5 cm wide, 25 cm. Check cloth 30 cm×30 cm. 38. 10g purple, yellow, green, blue and pink gradation. Pink cloth 30 cm×30 cm. Ribbon 2.5 cm wide, 12 cm. 1 golden bead. 39. Loose twisted crochet cotton (thick type) 20g white, 18 golden beads. Ribbon 2.5 cm wide, 40 cm. Lace 3.5 cm wide, 17 cm. Check cloth 30 cm×30 cm. Kapok. Steel crochet hook D (2.0 mm)

Finished size: Refer to chart.

Instructions: Make a round cushion in same manner as heart- shaped one.

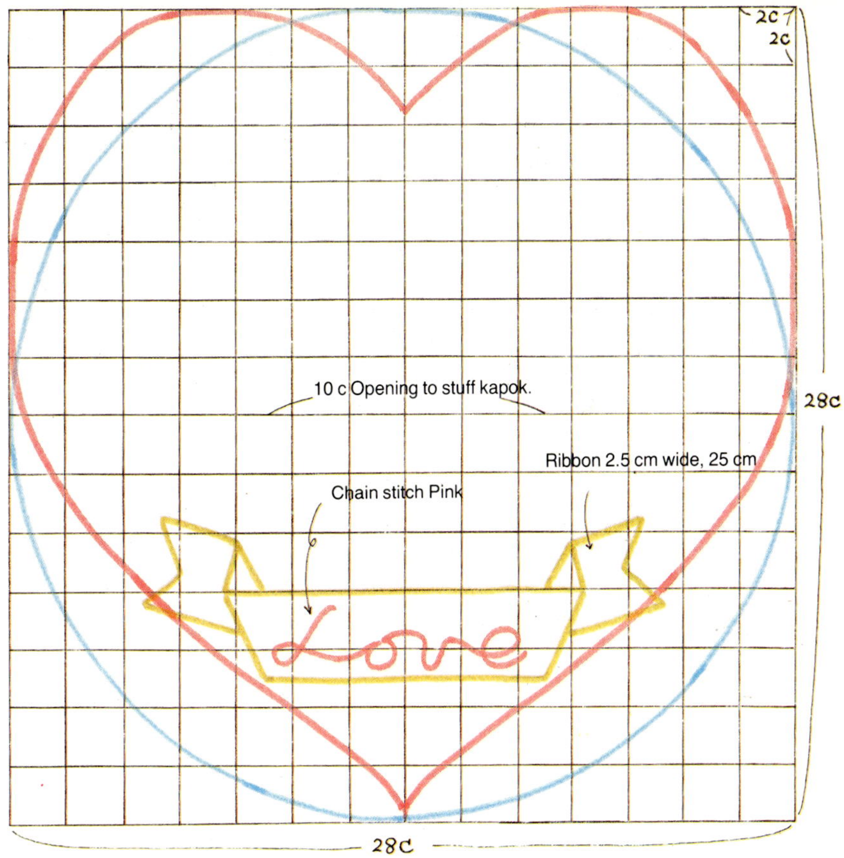

39 Flower 18 pieces

37 Braid

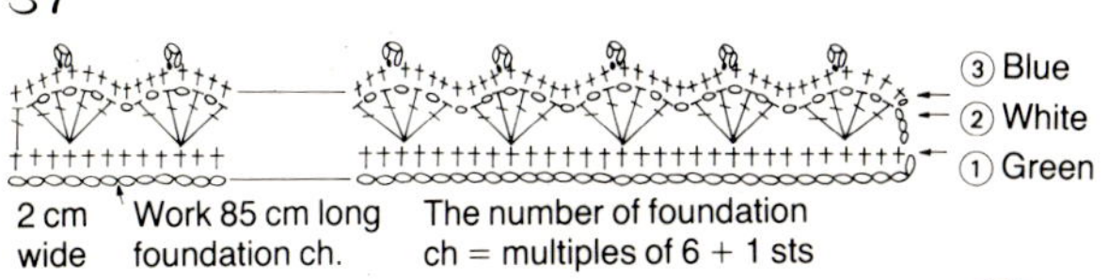

38 Braid

Work flower motifs same as No. 39.

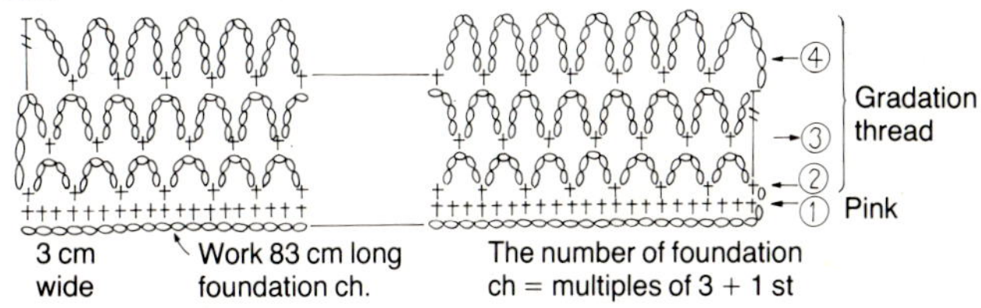

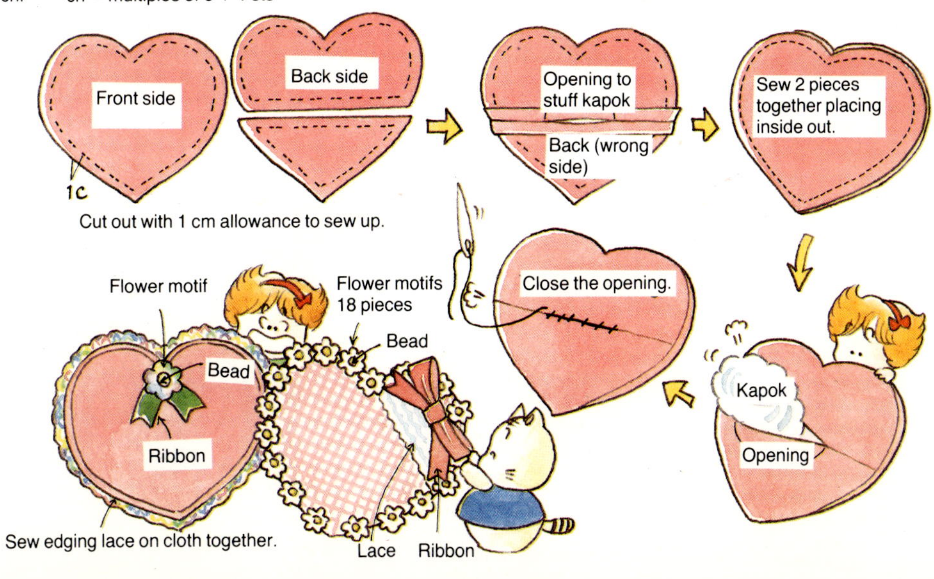

Edging

34–36 Rattan baskets become refreshed with pink braid. Attractive handy basket and pin-cushion for your own.
Designed by Misuko Nomura.
Instructions on page 24.

Edging

37–39 Dreamy petit cushions are trimmed with well-matched crochet lace. Put girlish frill, net st and flower motifs on.
Designed by Hitomi Tamura.
Instructions on page 25.

37

38

39

• Smart pochettes

Pochette

40. Delicate sense of pochette

Shown on page 29.

You'll need: DMC art 980 COTON LUSTRE C.B. 15g pink (8739). Ribbon 0.5 cm wide, 13 cm. Small flower lace. 1 snap button. Pink satin 17 cm×34 cm. Steel crochet hook D (2.0 mm).

Finished size: 15 cm in diameter.

Instructions: Rows 1–3: Work referring to chart. Row 4: Ch 3 at the beginning, 2-dc cluster and repeat around with "ch 5, 3-dc cluster, ch 5, 7 dc". Rows 5–8: Work net st increasing the number of ch. Work another piece until row 8. Put one piece upon another right side out and work together from row 9 except opening. Sew up a inner bag and join with lace. Work double ch st with 2 strands for string and attach on the back of both sides of opening. See page 32 to make a inner bag.

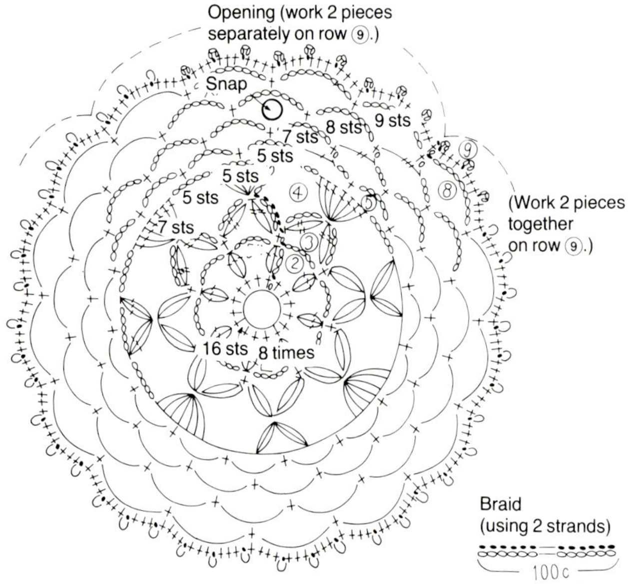

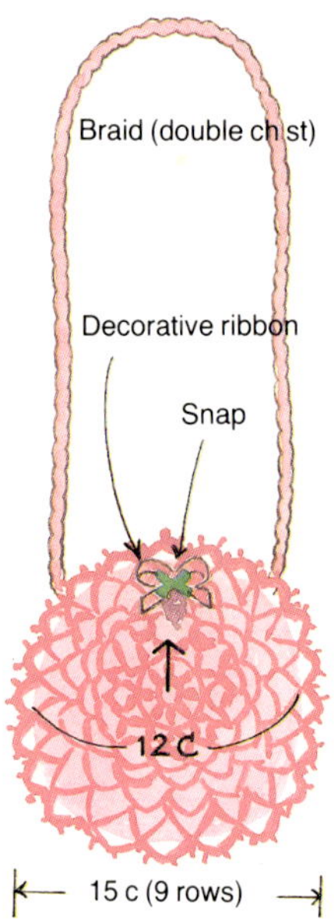

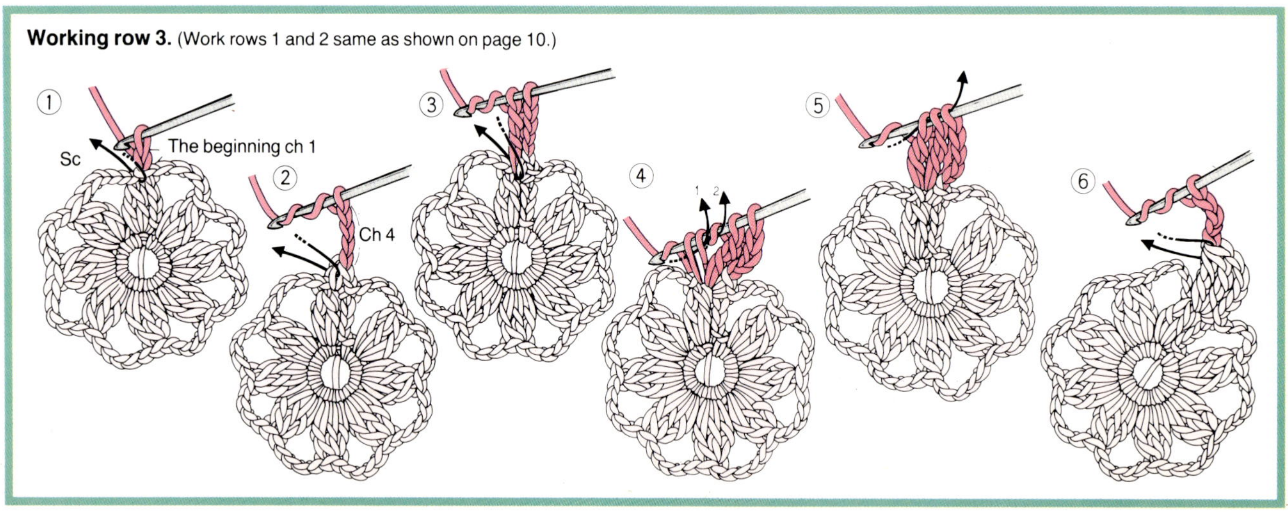

Pochette

40 Light pink of a wild rose is so tender and romantic. Make a fine pochette using such color. Designed by Mayumi Kawai. Instructions on page 28.

40

42 Pochette with wooden beads

Shown on page 31.

You'll need: DMC art 980 COTON LUSTRE C.B. 25g off-white (Ecru Nat.) 15 wooden beads 0.8 cm in diameter. Orange satin 18 cm×36 cm. Steel crochet hook D (2.0 mm).

Finished size: 16 cm in diameter.

Instructions: Row 1: Work 12 sc in a loop. Row 2: Ch 1 at the beginning and repeat "1 sc, ch 14" 11 times and then work 1 sc, ch 7, tr tr. Row 3: Work around with ch 8 and 1 sc. Row 4: Repeat "ch 8, 1 sc, ch 4, 2-tr cluster, ch 4, 1 sc" 11 times and work ch 4, 3-tr cluster. Rows 5-8: Work net st increasing the number of ch st. Row 9: Repeat around with "1 sc, 13 tr". Work another piece in same manner until row 9. Put one piece upon another right side out and join 2 pieces together with sc on row 10 except opening. Make loops for button on each side and put wooden beads on each side only for opening. See page 32 to make an inner bag.

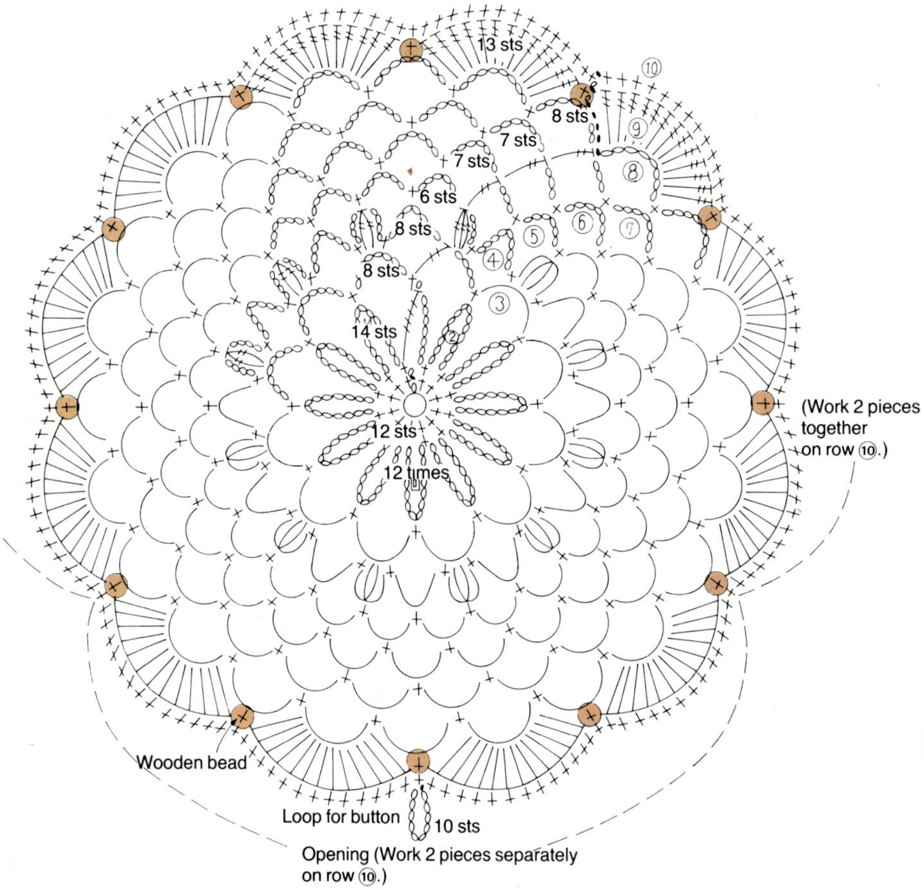

String (using 2 = 3 strands)

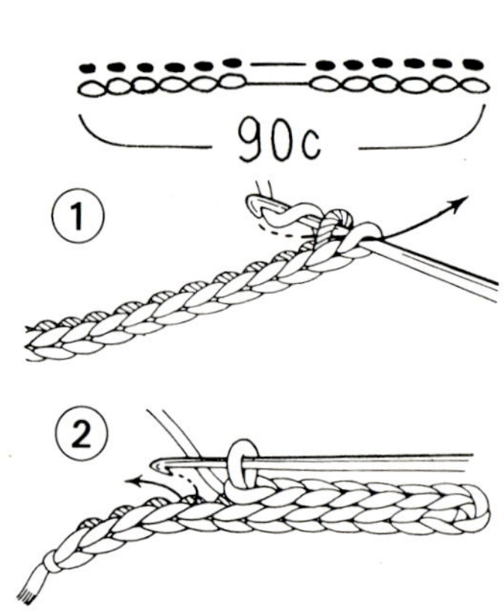

Working row 5 of the work No. 41. (Work the beginning ch same as shown on page 10.)

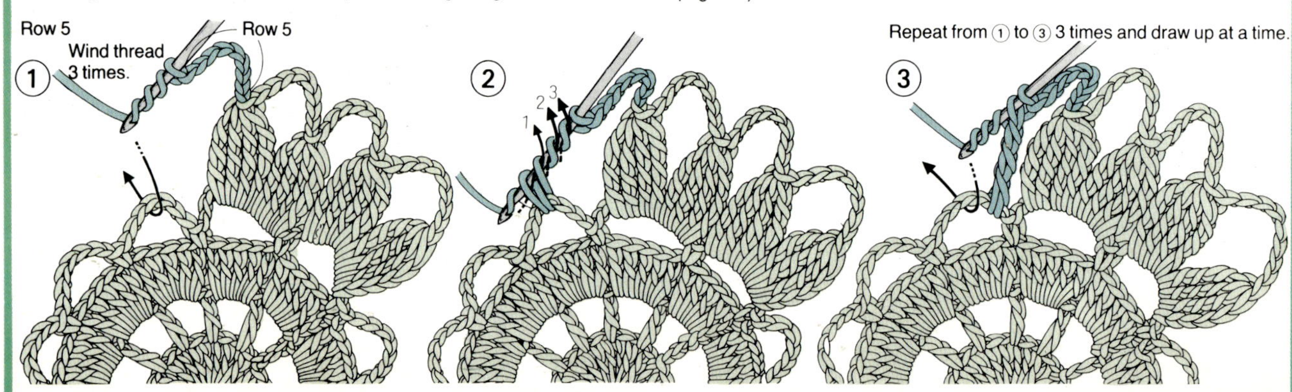

Pochette

41 Cool and refreshing emerald green. Cute six-cornered pochette.
Designed by Sakiko Honma.
Instructions on page 50.
42 Bright and delightful pochette like a sunflower. The accent is green wooden beads.
Designed by Sakiko Honma.
Instructions on page 30.

42

41

43 Pochette in vivid color

Shown on page 33.

You'll need: Loose twisted crochet cotton (thick type) 40g yellow (8725). 1 button 1 cm in diameter. Yellow satin 16 cm×29 cm. Steel crochet hook F (3.0 mm) and a 3.5 mm hook.

Finished size: 14 cm×14 cm.

Instructions: Row 1: Work the beginning ch 3 in a loop, 2 dc and repeat "ch 3, 3 dc" 3 times, ch 3 and sl st at the end. Row 2: Ch 3 and repeat "3 dc, ch 3, 3 dc" 3 times, 3 dc, ch 3, 2 dc and sl st at the end. Rows 3-6: Work increasing the number of times of 3 dc. Work another piece in same manner until row 6. Put 1 piece upon another right side out and work 2 pieces together on row 7 except opening. Work double ch st with 2 strands for string and attach on the back of both sides of opening. Make an inner bag as shown below.

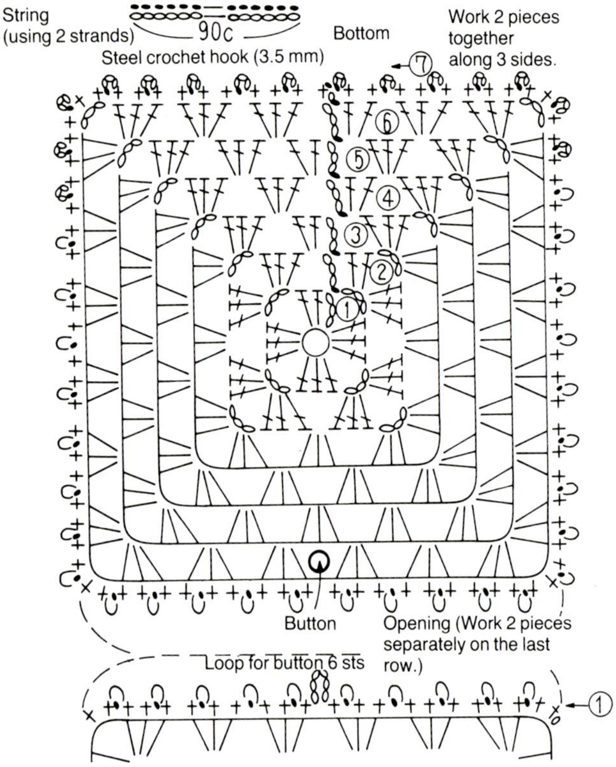

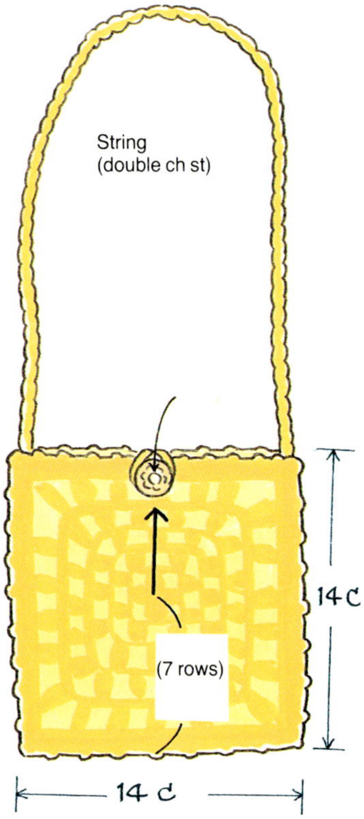

43

Pochette

43 Vivid yellow pochette is easy to make with basic motifs, complete with lovely picots for edging.
Designed by Sakiko Honma.
Instructions on page 32.

Pochette

44, 45 As it takes only a short time to make these pochettes with pearl beads or otherwise, work with various colors for your friends.
Designed by Mayumi Kawai.
Instructions on page 36.

46, 47 Use your favorite color and decorate with frill. These are little elaborate works.
Designed by Eiko Tobinai.
Instructions of No. 46 on page 37 and No. 47 on page 40.

44 Mini pochette Shown on page 34.

You'll need: DMC art 980 COTON LUSTRE C.B. 15g cream (8764). 44 cream beads 0.4 cm in diameter. Cream satin 15 cm×30 cm. Steel crochet hook D (2.0 mm).
Finished size: 13 cm×13 cm.
Instructions: Work in same way as No. 45 from rows 1 to 5. Row 6: Join thread in the corner shown in chart and ch 1 at the beginning then repeat "1 sc (1 dc, sl st-picot with 3-ch, ch 1) 2 times, 1 dc, sl st picot with 3-ch". Join 2 motifs together with sc right side out on row 6 of the second motif. Work 2 pieces separately for opening. Fasten beads on row 2 of the front side motif. Make 34-cm-long string with 4 strands working ch st and attach on the back of both sides of opening. Thread beads and fasten referring to chart. See page 32 to make a inner bag.

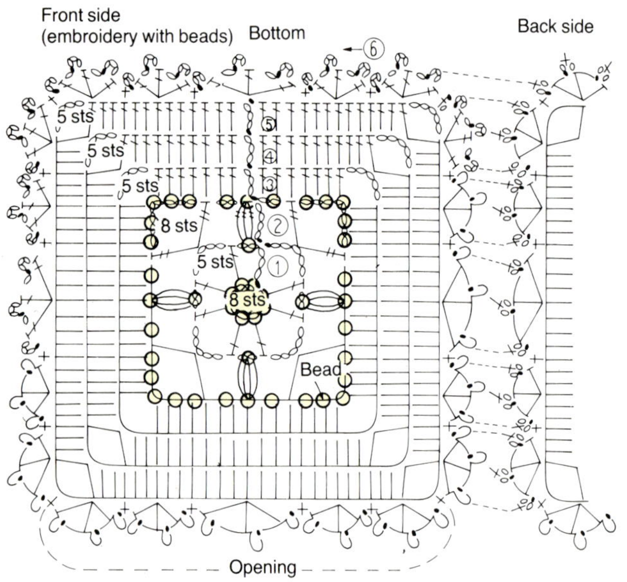

Joining on row 6 (sc)

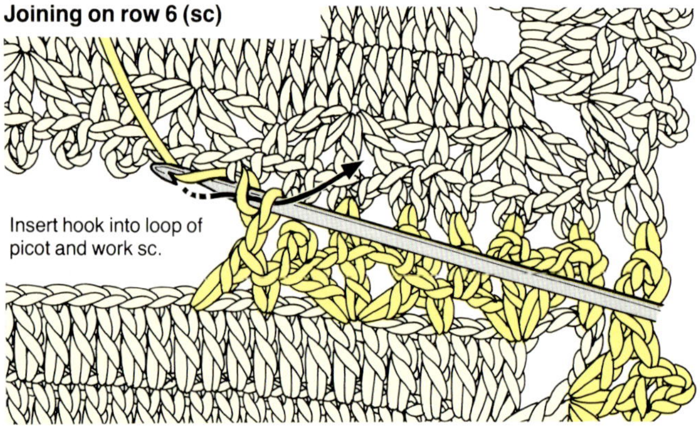

45 Mini pochette Shown on page 34.

You'll need: DMC art 980 COTON LUSTRE C.B. 20g green (8736). 1 pearl button 0.8 cm in diameter. Pale green satin 16 cm×32 cm. Steel crochet hook D (2.0 mm).
Finished size: 14 cm×14 cm.
Instructions: Make ch 8 to form ring. Row 1: Ch 3 at the beginning and repeat "ch 2, 1 dc, ch 5, 1 dc". Row 2: Work ch 4, 3-tr cluster and repeat "ch 2, 1 tr, ch 8, 1 tr, ch 2, 4-tr cluster". Rows 3-6: Work increasing the number of dc and work ch 5 at each corner. Work another piece in same manner until row 6. Put 1 piece upon another right side out and work 2 pieces together inserting hook into same st except opening. Make string working double ch st with 2 strands and attach. See page 32 to make an inner bag.

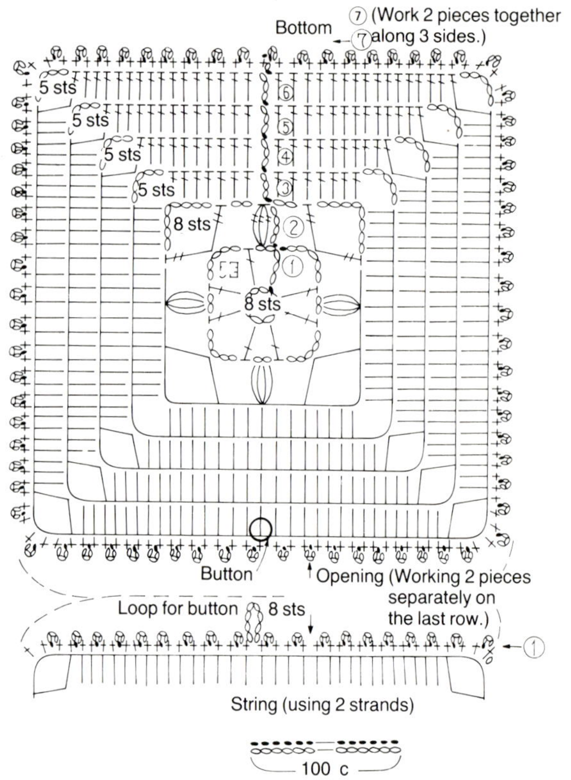

46 Sweet pochette with frill

Shown on page 35.

You'll need: Loose twisted crochet cotton (thick type) 50g pink (8771). Steel crochet hook F (3.0 mm)
Finished size: 20 cm×15 cm.
Instructions: Work ch 41 to form ring. Row 1: Ch 3 at the beginning and work 19 dc, 3-dc cluster (center), 20 dc. Rows 2-12: Work 2 dc in 1 dc of previous row at both sides and 3-dc cluster in the center dc of previous row. On front side, work sl st-picot with 5-ch at center as shown in chart. Put front upon back piece right side out and join 2 pieces together working backward with the variation of sc, facing front side. Work 2 pieces separately along opening and make a loop for button on back side as shown in chart. To make a button, work ch 5 to form ring and around with sc, hdc and dc referring to chart. Stuff cotton and pass thread on the last row then pull. Make string working ch st with 2 strands and attach on the back of both sides of opening.

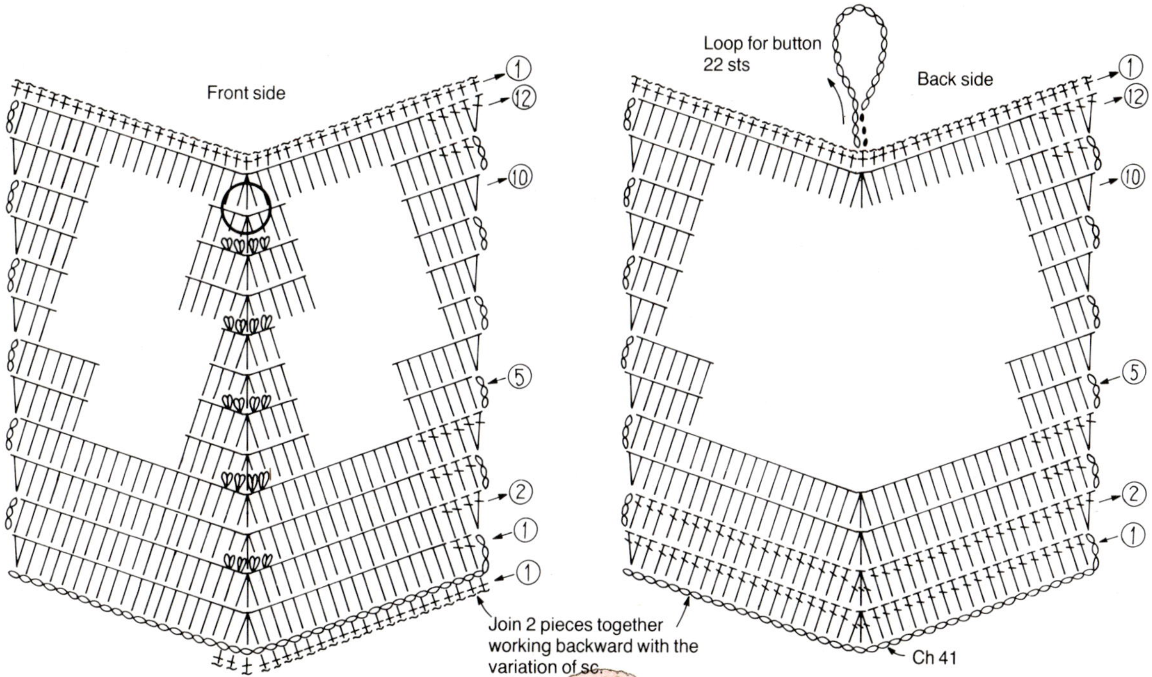

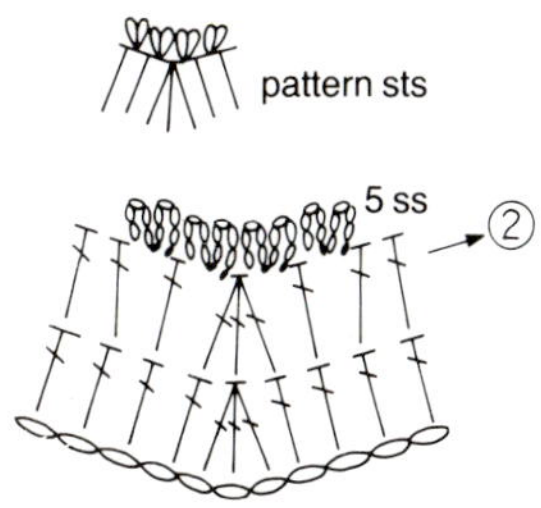

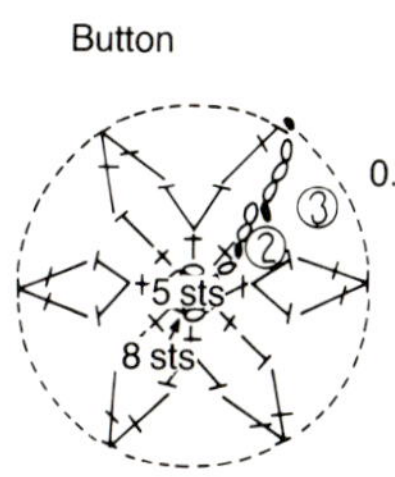

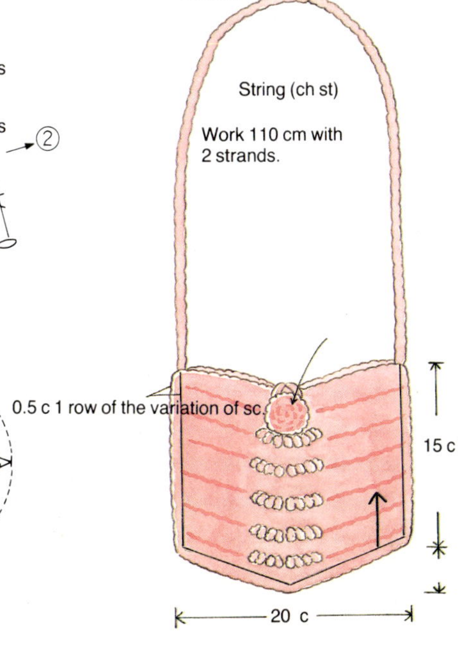

Fantasic lace with only 10g

Fantasy

48–51 You can make such a wonderful doily using only one 10g ball. It is a good idea to make with various colors and to hang on a wall or set in a frame. Designed by Misuko Nomura. Instructions on pages 40 and 41.

48

49

51
50

48·50 Mini doily with only 10g

Shown on pages 38 and 39.

You'll need: 48. 10g purple (8711). 50. 10g yellow (8725). Steel crochet hook D (2.0 mm).
Finished size: 17 cm in diameter.
Instructions: Work Nos. 48 and 50 in same manner. Work ch 10 to form ring. Row 1: Work ch 1 at the beginning, 22 sc and sl st at the end. Row 2: Ch 3 and repeat "ch 11, 1 dc" 10 times and ch 11. Row 3: Ch 1 and repeat around with "3 sc, ch 7". Rows 4-8: Work net st increasing the number of ch. Row 9: Work 5 tr between net st, 11 times. Row 10: Work around with "ch 7, 1 sc". Row 11: Ch 1 and repeat "1 sc, 6 dc, ch 3" around.

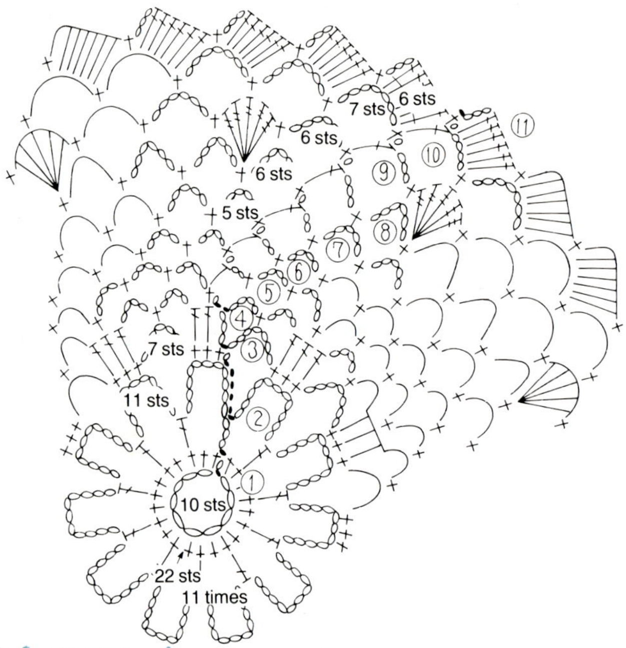

47 Pure white pochette

Shown on page 35.

You'll need: Loose twisted crochet cotton (thick type) 70g white. Steel crochet hook E (2.5 mm).
Finished size: 17 cm×17 cm.
Instructions: Front side Row 1: Work the beginning ch 3 and 11 dc in a loop. Row 2: Work sl st-picot with 5-ch between sc at the positions shown in chart and ch 2 at each corner. Row 3: Work around with sc. Rows 4 and 5: Work dc. Rows 6 and 7: Work in same as rows 2 and 3. Row 8: Work around with dc. Row 9: Work with dc but sc at each corner. Row 10-14: Work dc forming 4 sides as shown in chart and extending thread to the next row. Back side Make the foundation ch 35 and work dc until row 18. Put front upon back piece right side out and join both sides together working backward with the variation of sc, then join bottom with sl st. Make string with double ch st and attach the back of both sides of opening.

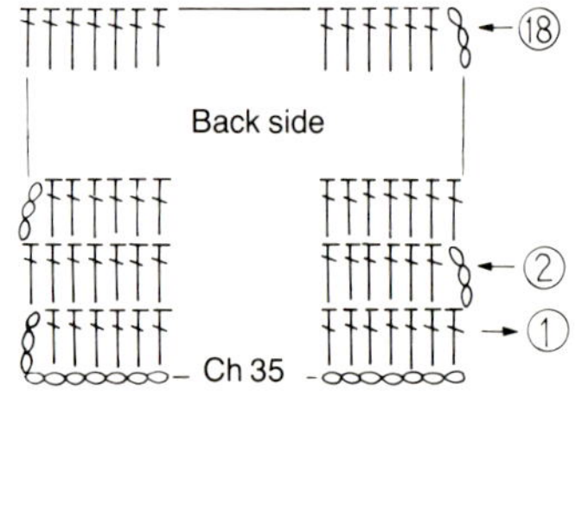

49·51 Mini doily with only 10g

Shown on pages 38 and 39.

You'll need: 49. 10g blue (8773). 51. 10g pink (8739). Steel crochet hook D (2.0 mm).
Finished size: 18 cm in diameter.
Instructions: Work ch 6 to form ring. Row 1: Work ch 1 at the beginning and 12 sc. Row 2: Ch and repeat "1 sc, ch 8" 5 times and work 1 sc, ch 3, 1 tr. Row 3: Ch 1 and repeat "3 sc, ch 4" 5 times and work 3 sc, ch 2, 1 hdc. Rows 4–12: Increase the number of ch and sc to shift sts of sc to the right. Rows 13–15: Increase the number of dc on sc of previous row and work net st on ch. Row 16: Ch 1 and repeat "(1 sc, ch 5) 10 times, 1 sc, ch 5, 2 dc, ch 3, 2 dc, ch 5" around.

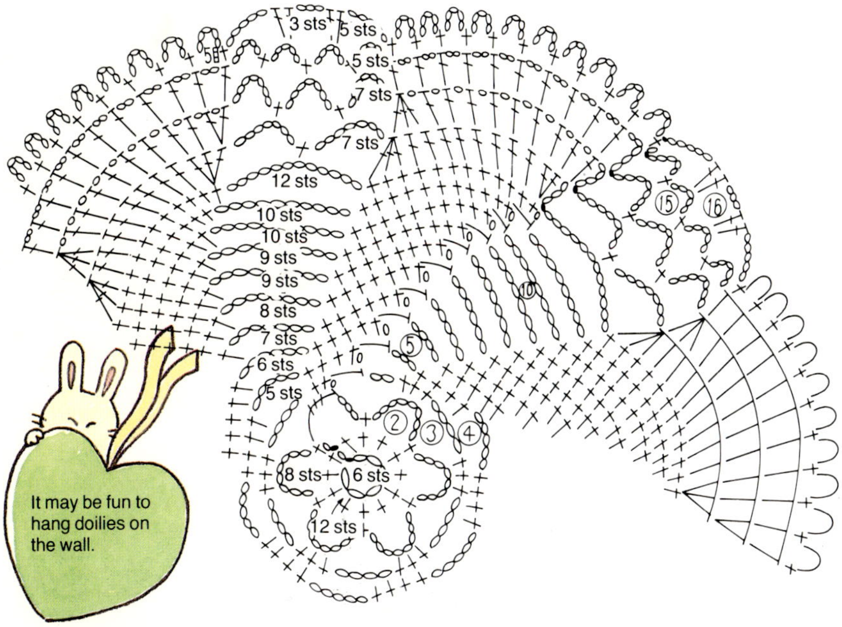

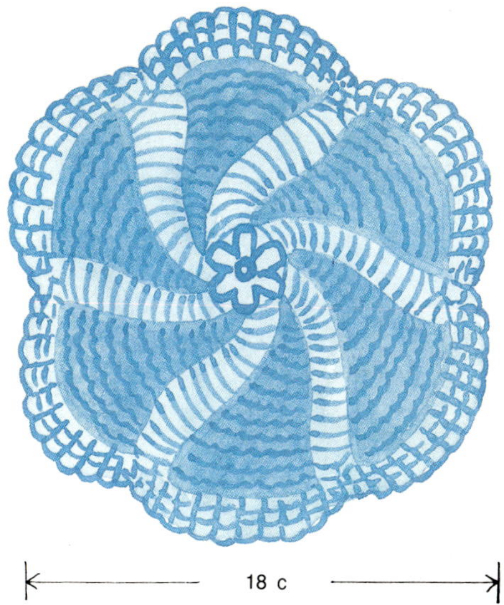

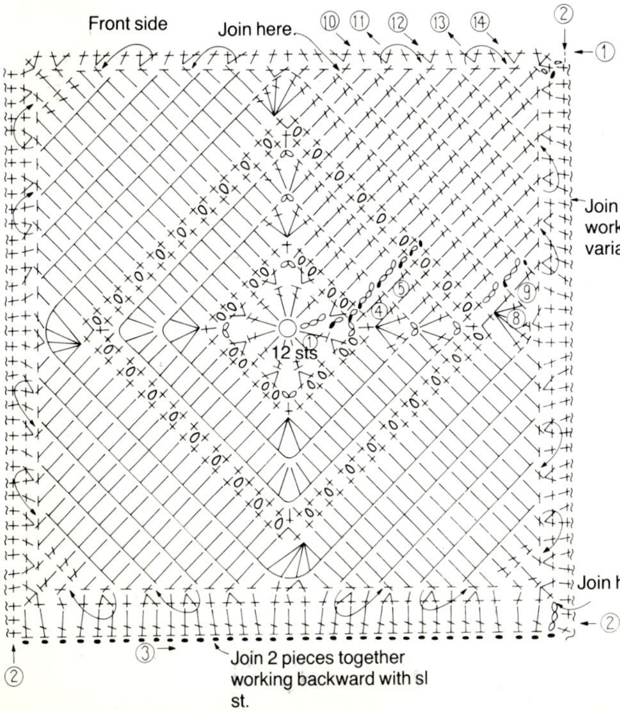

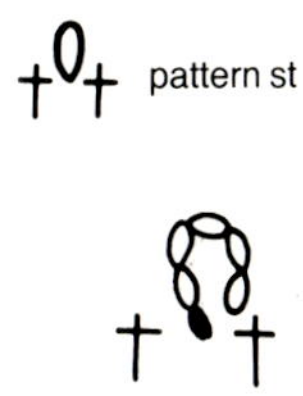

String

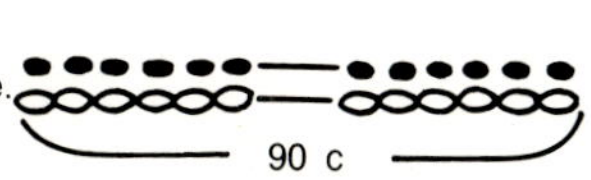

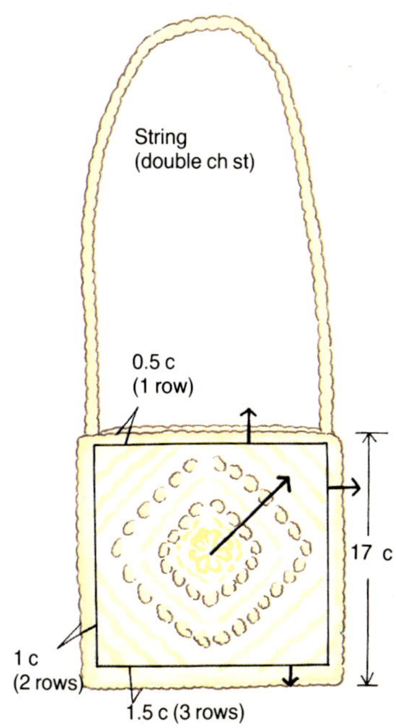

Softcolor

• Dreamy doily

52 Star-shaped doily

Shown on page 43.

You'll need: DMC art 980 COTON LUSTRE C.B. 40g saffron pink (8717). Steel crochet hook No. 10 (1.25 mm).

Finished size: Row 1: Work ch 3 at the beginning, 17 dc in a loop and sl st to form ring. Row 2: Ch 3, 2 dc and repeat "ch 3, 3 dc" 5 times and work ch 3, sl st to form ring. Rows 3-5: Work same as row 2 increasing sts. Rows 6-21: Make 6 diamond patterns. Row 22: Ch 3 and repeat around with "sl-st picot with 3-ch, ch 3, 1 dc".

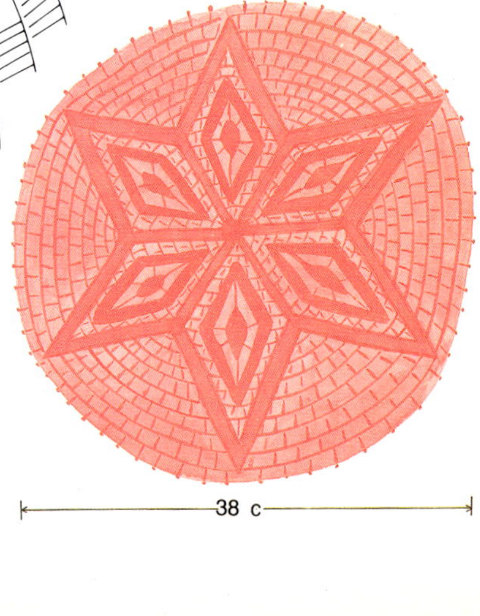

Softcolor

52 Star-shaped doily
Designed by Sonoe Hirata.
Instructions on page 42.

53 Gorgeous pineapple pattern doily

Shown on page 46.

You'll need: DMC art 980 COTON LUSTRE C.B. 30g white. Steel crochet hook D (2.0 mm).
Finished size: 31 cm in diameter.
Instructions: Work ch 10 to form ring. Row 1: Ch 4 at the beginning and repeat "ch 2, a tr" 15 times, ch 2 and sl st at the end. Row 2: Ch 3, and repeat "ch 2, 1 dc" 3 times, ch 2 and sl st at the end. Rows 3–9: Work same as row 2 increasing the number of ch and dc referring to chart. Rows 10–19: Make 8 pineapple patterns and work fan-shaped patterns between pineapples. Row 20: Ch 3, 1 dc and repeat around with "(ch 5, 2 dc, sl st-picot with 3-ch) 8 times, ch 5, 2 dc, sl st-picot with 3-ch, 2 dc".

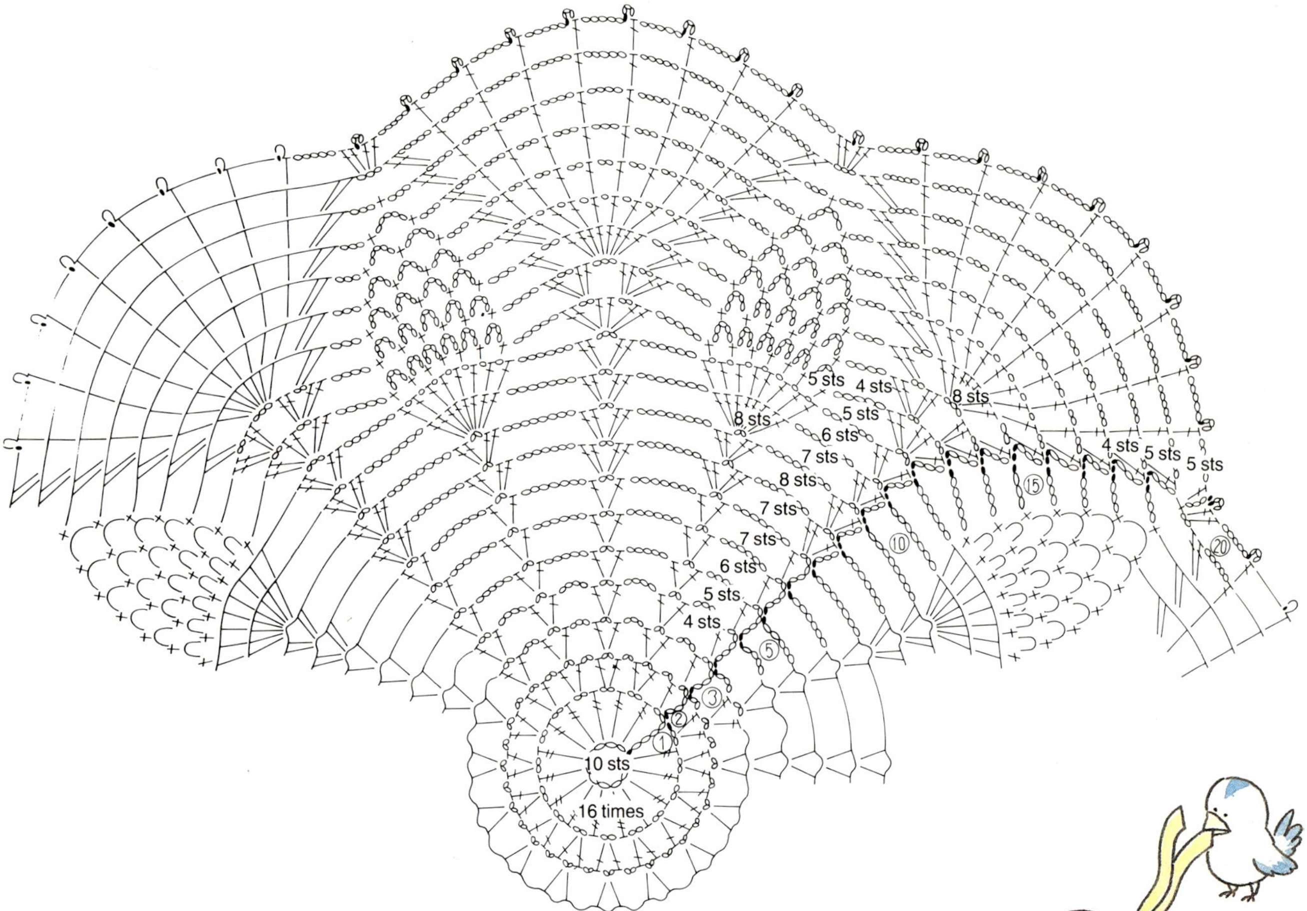

54 Gorgeous pineapple pattern doily

Shown on page 47.

You'll need: DMC at 980 COTON LUSTRE C.B. 20g cream (8764). Steel crochet hook D (2.0 mm).
Finished size: 32 cm in diameter.
Instructions: Work ch 6 to form ring. Row 1: Work ch 3 at the beginning, 19 dc and sl st at the end. Rows 2-10: Work net st increasing the number of ch. Row 11: Work ch 3, 1 dc, ch 2, 2 dc and repeat "ch 6, 2 dc, ch 2, 2 dc" around. Rows 12-19: Make 12 pineapple patterns. Row 20: Work ch 3 at the beginning, 1 dc, ch 2, 2 dc and repeat around with "2 dc, ch 2, 2 dc, (ch 5, sl st-picot with 3-ch, ch 5, 1 sc) 4 times, ch 5, sl st-picot with 3-ch, ch 5, 2 dc, ch 2, 2 dc".

32 c

53

Softcolor

53, 54 Everybody longs for such gorgeous pineapple pattern doilies.
Designed by Hideko Nagashima.
Instructions on pages 44 and 45.

54

To finish crochet lace neatly

To finish your patient work perfectly, there is one more step.

Instruments for finishing work

① Ironing board ② Iron ③ Cover cloth (white cotton) ④ Finishing paper (kraft paper or the like) ⑤ Transparent vinyl ⑥ Marking pins or finishing pins for handicraft ⑦ Sprayer ⑧ Detergent ⑨ Spray starch

Check points before finishing work

① Did you cut the end or beginning of thread neatly?
② Did you cut the thread tied and joined midway of the work?
③ Are there soilage or spots?

● If the work is soiled

Dissolve detergent in tepid water. Wash the work, shaking or squeezing softly. Rinse it repeatedly until the water becomes clear and apply starch, then wrap it in a towel to dry. Put finishing paper on the ironing board. Place vinyl over it, turn the work over on it and pin it. Dry it in a shaded, airy location. When it is 80-percent dry, finish with the iron.

● When there are spots on the fabrics

If it is a small spot, place the work on a towel and tap it with a cloth soaked in soap solution. Spots will be removed by changing the position of the towel and tapping repeatedly. If spots cannot be removed easily, soak the work in a solution of 1 liter water and 10g detergent. Boil the pieces for 10 minutes to 1 hour, depending on the spots. The rest of the procedure is the same as "If the work is soiled".

Finishing with iron

The finished sizes of works indicated here are those measured after they are stretched and finished by ironing. Therefore, the crocheted size is smaller than the finished size. Crochet lace is more beautiful when stretched and fixed. If the size of your work differs too much from the finished size indicated here, draw a bigger circle than the work and pin it accordingly.

● How to draw guidelines

If your work is round, draw a circle on paper according to the finished size. Divide the radius into 3 to 5 parts and draw inner circles depending on the size of the work. Then, draw dividing lines (radii) according to the number of patterns made radially. If there are not enough lines, you will not be able to decide the positions. On the other hand, it may become difficult to identify the stress on a pattern if there are too many lines. To finish other shapes, decide how many lines to draw based on the number of patterns.

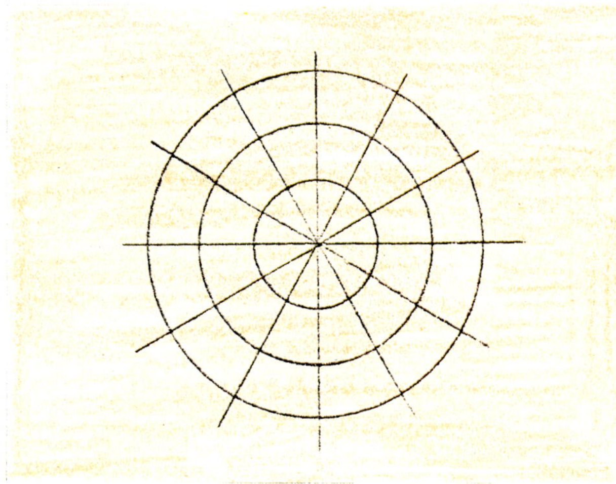

● How to pin the work

Turn the work over and put it on the guideline paper. First, pin at the center. Pin the work according to the guideline, pulling carefully. Setting the work neatly, divide it into smaller parts with pins. Pay attention to design, such as straight or curved lines of patterns. When the work is evenly stretched, remove the center pin before ironing.

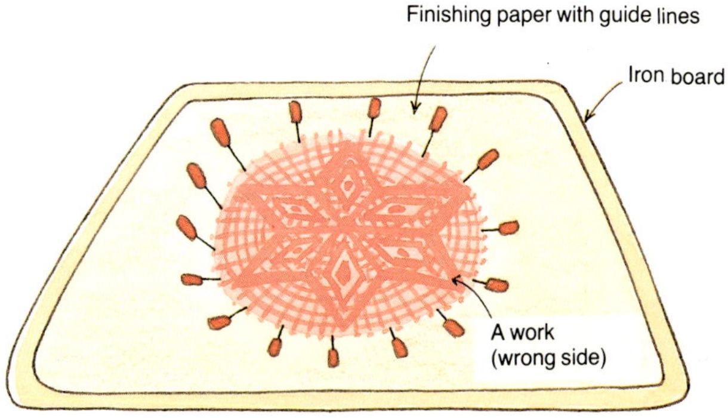

● Ironing

Spray water over the work and adjust the warp of stitches and the shape of picot or net. Spray starch and apply cover cloth. Press it from above with an iron set to high temperature to fix stitches. But be careful not to scorch the work. Remove pins after the work is completely dry.

When you wish to finish the work without using an iron, apply pins and spray starch, then dry with a dryer.

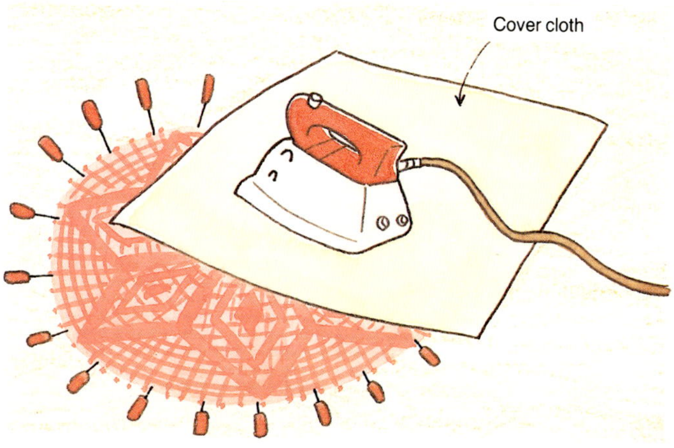

41 Cute six-cornered pochette

Shown on page 31.

You'll need: Loose twisted crochet cotton (thick type) 25g green (2909). 1 button 1 cm in diameter. Green satin 34 cm×20 cm. Steel crochet hook D (2.0 mm).

Finished size: 15 cm×18 cm.

Instructions: Row 1: Work ch 3 at the beginning, 23 dc in a loop and sl st to form ring. Row 2: Ch 3 and repeat "ch 3, 1 dc". Row 3: Work 5 dc inserting hook into 3-ch loop of the previous row. Row 4: Ch 1 and repeat "1 sc, ch 7". Row 5: Work ch 5 at the beginning, 3-dtr cluster and repeat around with "ch 9, 4-dtr cluster". Rows 6-7: Work net st making 6 patterns. Work another piece until row 8 and work 2 pieces separately along opening, then work one more row for opening. Work cord st and attach on the back of both sides of opening.

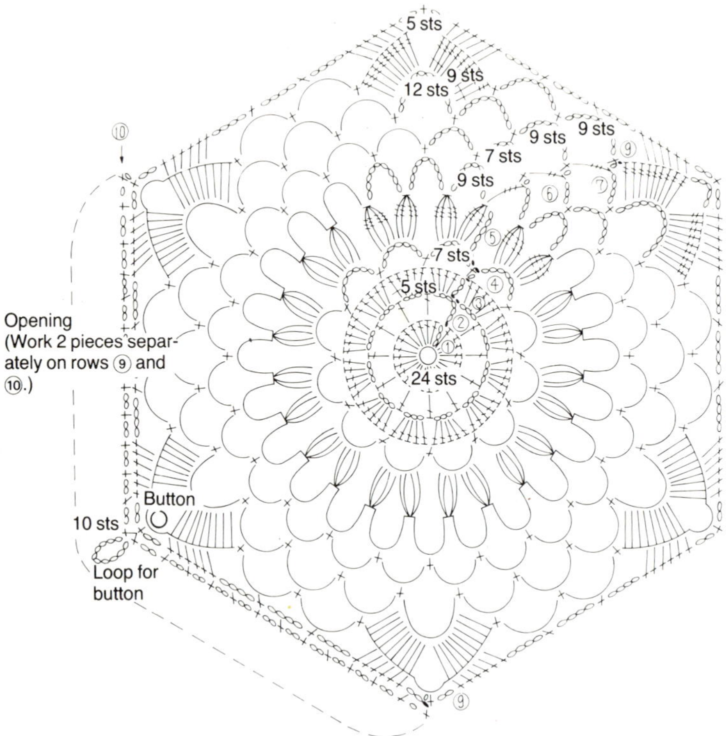

Cord st 90 cm long with 2 strands

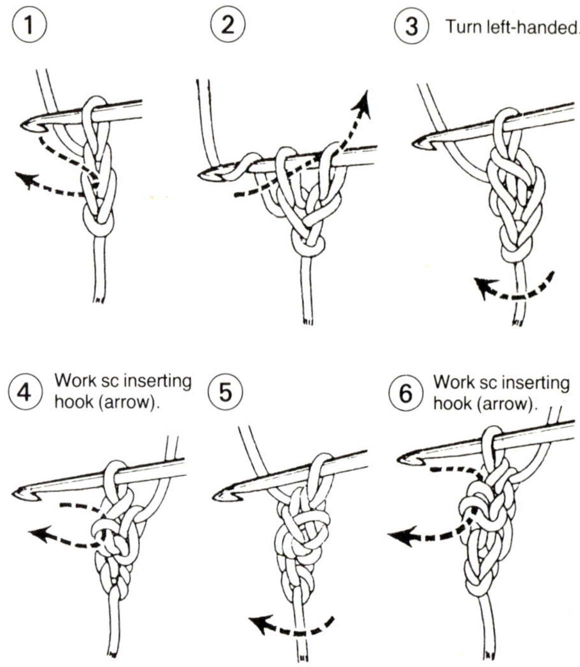

22

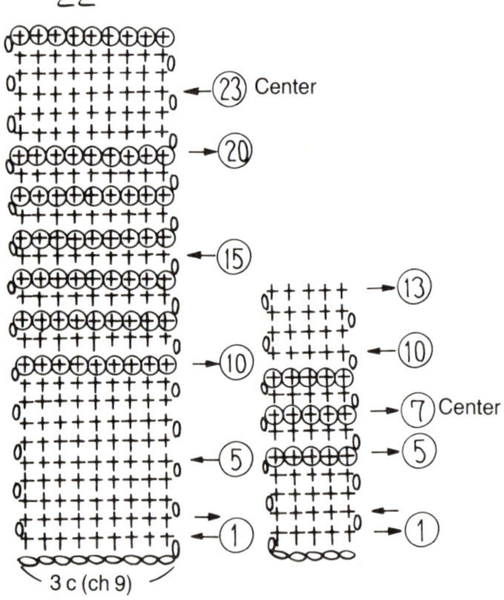

23

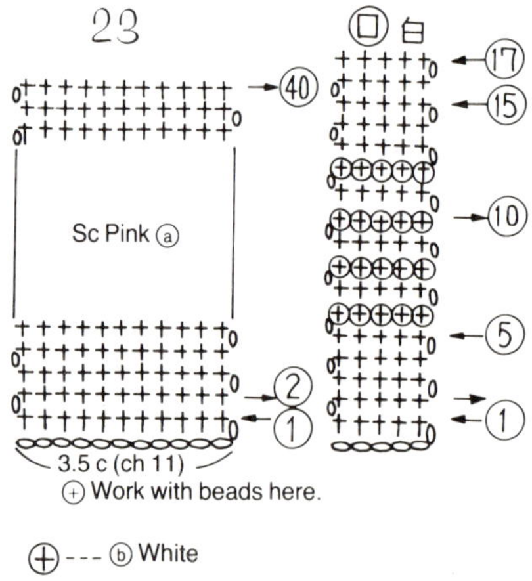

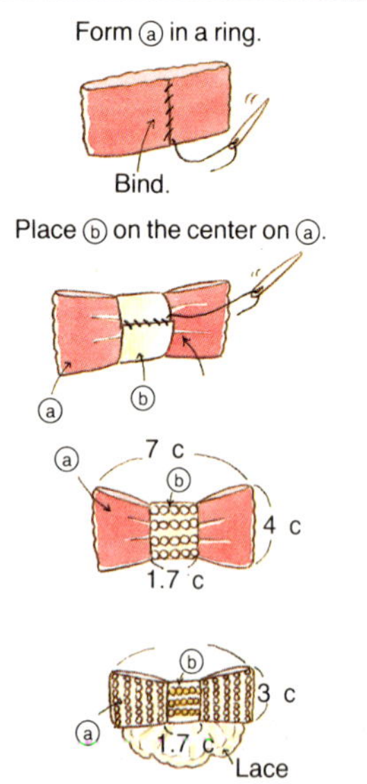